Studies in Liturgical Musicology
Edited by Dr. Robin A. Leaver

"THE WAY TO HEAVENS DOORE"

An Introduction to Liturgical Process and Musical Style

by

STEVEN PLANK

Studies in Liturgical Musicology, No. 2

The Scarecrow Press, Inc.
Lanham, Md., & London

British Library Cataloguing-in-Publication Data available

Library of Congress Cataloging-in-Publication Data

Plank. Steven, 1951–
   "The way to heavens doore" : an introduction to liturgical process and
musical style / By Steven Plank.
       p.   cm. — (Studies in liturgical musicology ; no. 2)
   Includes bibliographical references (p.   ) and index.
   ISBN 0–8108–2953–3 (acid-free paper)
   1. Church music. 2. Liturgics. I. Title. II Series.
ML3000.P53 1994
781.71—dc20   94–34082

Church–musick

Sweetest of sweets, I thank you: when displeasure
Did through my bodie wound my minde,
You took me thence, and in your house of pleasure
A daintie lodging me assign'd.

Now I in you without a bodie move,
Rising and falling with your wings:
We both together sweetly live and love,
Yet say sometimes, God help poore Kings.

Comfort, 'Ile die; for if you poste from me,
Sure I shall do so, and much more:
But if I travell in your companie,
You know the way to heavens doore.

George Herbert
The Temple (1633)

CONTENTS

Editor's Preface

THE role of music in liturgical worship is frequently misunderstood. Both musicians and clergy often make the mistake of considering music as an optional extra, an element that is not really fundamental to the essence of the liturgy. This allows musicians to concentrate solely on the "performing" aspects of worship without troubling themselves with understanding the theological principles and liturgical imperatives of worship. Similarly, it allows clergy to assume that they have no need to understand the musical aspects of worship, except for music's basic propaganda value. But the premise is a false one. Far from being a peripheral concern, music is fundamental to most forms of worship. Even exceptions such as the tradition based on Zwingli's liturgical formulations, or the later Quaker tradition of worship, have subsequently adopted musical forms.

Music has been an essential part of the process of liturgical development, indeed, music has often given the impetus to liturgical formation. In the worship of Israel, music was fundamental to the offering of sacrifice.[1] The early Christian Fathers, when speaking about worship, frequently refer to the fact that in the singing of psalms the music creates a unity in the congregation: its members sing "as with one voice."[2] It is the changing melodies of Gregorian chant that express and mark the changing seasons and celebrations of the church year. In the medieval period, it is the polyphonic *cantus firmus* mass, in which all the settings of the Ordinary are based on the same melody, that provides an overall unity that the liturgy would

1. See John W. Kleinig, *The Lord's Song: The Basis, Function and Significance of Choral Music in Chronicles* (Sheffield: Sheffield Academic Press, 1993).
2. See, for example, the citations assembled by John A. Lamb, *The Psalms in Christian Worship* (London: Faith Press, 1962), 18–45.

not otherwise possess. Of the 49 pages of Luther's *Deutsche Messe* of 1526, approximately 27 are filled with musical notation, thus underlining the fact that Luther's liturgy cannot be understood without a consideration of its liturgical music. In Calvin's Genevan liturgy, *La Forme des Prières* of 1542, the singing of metrical psalms is not optional but rather essential, since at those points where such singing is prescribed the metrical psalm *is* the liturgy. Similarly, the hymns of Charles Wesley in many respects effectively became the liturgy for later Methodists.

It is this fundamental connection between liturgy and music, especially within the process of liturgical development, that forms the substance of this book. Steven Plank has written a useful introductory text that is representative rather than exhaustive in scope. Its primary purpose is to raise some of the issues and then to invite and encourage the reader to make further studies into the relationship between music and its functions within specific liturgical forms.

Steven Plank teaches musicology and Collegium Musicum at the Conservatory of Music, Oberlin College, and is an active participant in early music in general and church music in particular.

Robin A. Leaver
Series Editor
Westminster Choir College & Drew University

Author's Preface

IN a poem from *The Temple*, the English poet and cleric George Herbert (1593–1633) describes church music as "the way to heavens doore." The notion that the music of the liturgy possesses such a spiritual power is a familiar one, though one, I suspect, that has been most generally associated with affective "inspiration" or something akin to the "holiness of beauty." In the study pursued here, I aim to consider, by and large, different associations: namely, those that relate the particularities of musical style to specific spiritual processes taking place within the liturgy; to consider the liturgy as a dynamic set of actions, the nature of which helps shape musical style and is often felicitously served by it.

The first chapter seeks to survey the close relationship of liturgy and music in general, and to outline some of the historiographical underpinnings of the "process" view that I adopt here. Chapter Two investigates the temporal dimensions of liturgy—especially its circularity—and the establishment of ritual texts. A consideration of the Daily Office and the Mass follows in Chapters Three and Four, describing each liturgy not as a static collection of texts, but as a fluid sequence of events closely intertwined with questions of musical style. In Chapter Five the homiletic capacity of church music is examined with a look at the Restoration anthem and the eighteenth-century Lutheran cantata.

Interdisciplinary work such as The *Way to Heavens Doore* can often appropriately address diverse audiences. Here I have been chiefly mindful of two groups: music history students who seek a contextual understanding of their subject, and practitioners of church music who look to explore broader aspects of their vocation.

In the course of preparing this study, I have incurred debts of gratitude to many. As *The Way to Heavens Doore* does not intend to be a new documentary source study, I have made frequent use of the rich secondary literature on liturgical history. All students of liturgy, I suspect, must acknowledge a debt to Joseph Jungmann and Gregory Dix whose work is fundamental to the questions at hand, and moreover, often congenially so. In this particular case, the debt is an extensive one. James McKinnon's excellent anthology, *Music in Early Christian Literature*, has also been richly enabling, and quotations appear here with permission of the publisher, the Cambridge University Press.

My editor, Prof. Robin A. Leaver, long an inspiring figure in the field of liturgical musicology, has been an insightful critic and a patient guide. My colleague and friend the Revd. Dr. Arnold Klukas has similarly been a close reader of this material, offering many helpful suggestions along the way. For his sensitive eye for design and the computer processing of the text and musical examples I am grateful to Michael Lynn of Oberlin.

A number of the ideas here had their beginnings in my work with music history students at Oberlin College. I am grateful for the pleasure of their company over the years and the stimulation of their inquiring minds. One in particular gave a strong impetus to this book by lingering after class one day to ask, "Is there a book like...?"

The patient companionship of my wife, Katherine Straney Plank, has, as always, inspired, instructed, and sustained in ways beyond telling. This book is dedicated to Charles A. Plank and Joyce Clayton Plank, whose son it is my very good fortune to be.

Steven Plank
Oberlin College
Feast of Bl. William Tyndale, 1993

LIST OF EXAMPLES

ABBREVIATIONS

MECL   McKinnon, James. *Music in Early Christian Literature.* Cambridge: Cambridge University Press, 1987.

MRR   Jungmann, Joseph A. *The Mass of the Roman Rite: Its Origins and Development.* 2 vols. 1949. Eng. trans. New York: Benziger Bros., 1951.

SL   Dix, Gregory. *The Shape of the Liturgy.* 1945. New York: Seabury Press, 1982.

1

LITURGY AND MUSIC

THE theologian and poet Karl Plank draws a strong contrast between "we who have thinned the resounding of history to a tinny thud" and the poet who "discovers a resonant depth in the connections of lived experience."[1] These are valuable images for a study of liturgy and music; valuable not only for their inherent musicality, but moreover for their critique of a dehumanized history, be it of liturgy or of music. This study is impelled by the idea that a knowledge of liturgy helps restore the "connections" of musical experience, and a knowledge of music history similarly humanizes our view of liturgy.

To place music and liturgy together is an important task for the student of music history. In the West, the Christian church has been the arena in which notation, modality, rhythmic organization, and polyphony were developed and brought to fruition. Moreover, until the nineteenth century, the church provided the chief form of musical education for "professional" musicians in the form of chorister training. Even in the early conservatories such as the Pietà in Venice, Vivaldi and his female charges performed in liturgical or semiliturgical context. Once trained, the musician would find the church to be

---

1. Karl Plank, "Unbroken Trains: Reflections on Mike Martin's 'Approaching History'," unpublished paper presented at the Southeast Regional Meeting of the American Academy of Religion in Atlanta, March, 1991.

the major employer of musicians through the eighteenth century—even court patronage would often bring with it chapel duties.

More recently, liturgical forms such as the Ordinary of the Mass, Requiem, or Vespers have become standard musical essays and concert fare. Elements of a "concert liturgy" became standard in the seventeenth century, well represented by the aestheticism of works like Monteverdi's *Vespers of the Blessed Virgin Mary* (1610). Such works, however, still claim a liturgical context. Later, the concert element is retained and the liturgical context cast away. With this liberation, a free attitude to the text is taken as well, as in Brahms' *German Requiem,* Britten's *War Requiem,* or Bernstein's *Mass.* Bach's *Mass in B-minor* may provide an interesting transition between "concert liturgy" and "liturgical concert." Certain portions of the work, viz. the "Sanctus," were originally performed as part of the Leipzig liturgy in 1724, and 1726 or 1727. However, *in toto,* it defies a liturgical setting.

Finally, the majority of the surviving music in the West until the Renaissance is liturgical. This reflects in part the centrality of the church in the Middle Ages, but equally so the church's desire to codify and regularize, a concern not generally relevant to secular music making of the day.

As our understanding of music history requires an appreciation of its liturgical environment, so too does an understanding of liturgy necessitate a sensitivity to its musical voice. Music's symbiotic relation with liturgy derives from many factors and its contributions to the liturgy are diverse. Perhaps one of the oldest and most compelling is the idea that to sing something changes its nature, sets it apart. In this way the music, often acting to solemnify the text, removes the text from the mundane and consecrates the sonic world in which the liturgy takes place. As the sanctuary defines sacred space and as the liturgical calendar and daily round of offices consecrate the passing of time, so too does ritual singing sacralize the sound space of the text.[2] Music, too, powerfully enriches the affective content of the liturgy, giving both an outlet for and nurture to strong emotion. The first-century *Odes of Solomon* offer a good example:

> I poured out praise to the Lord
>   because I am his.

> I will pronounce his holy song,
>   because my heart is with him;

> For his cithara is in my hands,
>   and the songs of his rest shall not be still.
>   (Ode XXVI)[3]

In this instance it is a pious affection that impels the song. Throughout the course of liturgical history this pious affection will be in tension with the "aesthetic" quality of the music or music making *per se*. The "pleasure" of the music, for instance, rings clearly in Walter of Coincy's remarks:

> And all loved to sing
> The delightful kyrielles
> The sweet and lovely sequences
> With full voice and in rich tones.[4]

2. On the consecration of time and space, see the classic study by Mircea Eliade, *The Sacred and the Profane: the Nature of Religion* (New York: Harcourt Brace Jovanovich, 1959). In the magical tradition, which itself is often a parody of Christian liturgy, singing may not only set the text apart, but may in fact empower it, as in the concept of incantation.

3. Cited in James McKinnon, *Music in Early Christian Literature* [MECL] (Cambridge: Cambridge University Press, 1987), 24.

But at various times, one finds this pleasure to be a suspect strain. In the fourth century, Athanasius found singing for amenity "blameworthy."[5] And no instance of the conflict is more famous, I suspect, than Augustine's vacillation between aestheticism and pious hearing in his well-known *Confessions*:

> [W]hen I recall the tears which I shed at the song of the Church in the first days of my recovered faith, and even now as I am moved not by the song but by the things which are sung, when sung with fluent voice and music that is most appropriate, I acknowledge again the great benefit of this practice. Thus I vacillate between the peril of pleasure and the value of the experience, and I am led more...to endorse the custom of singing in church so that by the pleasure of hearing the weaker soul might be elevated to an attitude of devotion. Yet when it happens to me that the song moves me more than the thing which is sung, I confess that I have sinned blamefully and then prefer not to hear the singer. Look at my condition![6]

Explicit in Augustine's remarks is the concept that the pleasure of the music is an aid to the "weaker soul." At various times liturgical music functions evangelically as a sweet enticement to the rigors of religious exercise one might otherwise resist. Augustine's contemporary, John Chrysostom, underscores music as an enticement:

---

4. Cited in Jean Leclercq, OSB, *The Love of Learning and the Desire for God*, (New York: Fordham University Press, 1977), 292. Walter of Coincy was a 13th-cent. monk of St. Medard.

5. MECL, 53.

6. MECL, 155.

> When God saw that the majority of men were slothful, and that they approached spiritual reading with reluctance and submitted to the effort involved without pleasure...he mixed melody with prophecy, so that enticed by the rhythm and melody, all might raise sacred hymns to him with great eagerness.[7]

The idea is by no means restricted to early Christianity. For example, in the early seventeenth-century dedication of G. F. Anerio's *Teatro Armonico Spirituale* to the founder of the Oratorians, Philip Neri, and to St. Jerome, Orazio Griffi refers to the "sweet deception" of music as a lure to the exercises of the Oratory. The typical two-part construction of the oratorio, with a sermon in between the two halves, insured a "captive audience" for the preacher's exhortation.[8]

Yet another function of music in the liturgy is as unifier of corporate action. Several have argued strongly for corporate participation as a critical liturgical concept, although it is a varying factor in liturgical history.[9] But corporate intent is no guarantee of smooth group coordination. Music plays a large role in allowing the various orders to fulfill their discrete functions smoothly...together. Music, simply put, allows the many voices of the group to become one.[10] From a practical standpoint, this much is readily apparent. However, we should underscore that music, in uniting disparates into one, reflects

---

7. MECL, 80.

8. See Howard Smither, *A History of the Oratorio*, vol 1 (Chapel Hill: University of North Carolina Press, 1977), 121-122.

9. See especially Louis Bouyer, *Liturgical Piety* (Notre Dame: University of Notre Dame Press, 1955) and Gregory Dix, OSB, *The Shape of the Liturgy* [SL] (1945; New York: Seabury Press, 1982).

in itself a larger liturgical issue, viz. the bringing into (inner) harmony the various members of the group with each other and within themselves.

The Gospel of Matthew is strong in promoting the harmony of the worshipping body: "If you are offering your gift at the altar, and there remember that your brother has something against you, leave your gift there before the altar and go; first be reconciled to your brother, and then come and offer your gift."[11] Several modern writers are insightful in relating the liturgy to notions of inner harmony. Carl Jung, for example, observes: "[T]he mystery of the Eucharist transforms the soul of the empirical man, who is only a part of himself, into his totality, symbolically expressed by Christ. In this sense, therefore, we can speak of the Mass as the *rite of the individuation process*."[12] Similarly, Geoffrey Wainwright notes: "Singing is at home in the liturgy because worship bears, in Christianity as in other religions, the character of *dromenon*, a complex 'drama' of words and actions in which music may help to bring mental and physical activity together in unity or counterpoint."[13]

In this sense the individual's quest for holiness (psychologically a wholeness in which opposites are reconciled) mirrors

10. Cf. Nicetas of Remesiana, who suggested the analogy of the three young men in the fiery furnace (Daniel 3) who sang "in unison." See Joseph A. Jungmann, *Christian Prayer Through the Centuries* (1969; Eng. trans., New York: Paulist Press, 1978), 30.

11. Matthew 5: 23, 24.

12. Carl Jung, "Transformation Symbolism in the Mass," in *Psychology and Western Religion* (Princeton: Princeton University Press, 1984), 169.

13. Geoffrey Wainwright, *Doxology* (Oxford: Oxford University Press, 1980), 199.

the unity of the body of Christ, and this is a unity audibly pro-
claimed in one song, one voice. Moreover, music as an expression of harmony (variously defined) echoes the cosmic
harmony in which creation manifests order, rhythm, and rec-
onciliation.

And finally, music in the liturgy allows the worshipper a
knowledge of *Deus Creator*, in whose creative play the singing
worshipper can claim a share. Musical creativity shares in per-
petuating the act of creation and thus affords a particular
glimpse of God at work (or at play) in this way. Jean Leclercq
has brought to light numerous examples from scripture and
the Fathers in which the human referent to God is "artist."[14]
And this divine "artistry" becomes the model of our own; our
artistic creations, in a sense, "found" worlds, an echo of the
divine creative spirit and a means through which the divine
creative spirit remains active in creation.[15]

In summary, music and liturgy are intertwined in several
ways:

Music finds in the liturgy and in the church

  • the development and codification of major
    theoretical concerns

  • the major institution for the training and
    employment of musicians

14. See "*Otium Monasticum* as a Context for Artistic Creativity" in *Monasticism and the Arts* (Syracuse: Syracuse
University Press, 1984), 70.

15. Cf. Eliade, *Sacred and Profane*, 45: "[E]very construction or fabrication has the cosmogony as paradigmatic
model. The creation of the world becomes the archetype of
every human gesture, whatever its plane of reference may
be."

Liturgy employs music for

- setting ritual texts apart

- enriching the affective content

- sweetening the religious exercise

- unifying corporate action

- echoing cosmic harmony

- sharing in divine creation

It is this close intertwining that compels us to look at each in light of the other. But what "look" will we take? The nature of the "look" is important in determining the outcome of the view. Though liturgy readily becomes a "context" for music, and vice versa, the engagement of the "other" does not necessarily contextualize; does not necessarily lead us away from the "tinny thud of thinned history" to the "resonant depths of lived experience." The contextual approach adopted here must move beyond objective description to subjectively inflected understanding. Many have put forth convincing arguments that the work of art's meaning is not an autonomous, unvarying entity, but is rather to be found in the interplay it enjoys with its social environment.[16] And if this be true for music written as essentially a musical event—the work of art—how much more so for music written explicitly in the service of social ends, like the liturgy. The venerable Dom Gregory Dix writes that

16. Outstanding voices articulating this view include Walter Benjamin in his classic essay "The Work of Art in the Age of Mechanical Reproduction" in *Illuminations* (New York: Schocken Books,1968): 217-251. With regard to music, Gary Tomlinson's "The Web of Culture" *Nineteenth-Century Music* 7 (1984): 350-362 is *inter alia* a strong exposition of this idea.

the study of liturgy [or liturgical music] is not rightly to be regarded as a branch of canon law or Christian administrative history; it cannot be properly treated as the mere study of a series of changes in 'regulations' about Christian worship...We have forgotten that the study of liturgy is above all a study of *life*, that Christian worship has always been something done by real men and women....[17]

Accordingly, we must seek to understand the nexus of music and liturgy in terms of human processes that take us, as Morris Berman puts it, to the "center of the gushy interior."[18] In so doing we do not abdicate historical responsibility and replace it with personal fictive vision, but rather acknowledge that the historical event—liturgical, musical, or otherwise—has human dimensions that must also be taken into account if we are to get a sense of the thing that "really" happened; to find the living word among the dead letters of the text. History happened somatically, affectively, psychologically, and spiritually, and the tight constraints of unrelenting objectivity can impede our consideration of history so defined. The task at hand is an interpretative one in which an observant objectivity seeks the counterpoint of subjective discernment.

In what follows, specific liturgical forms, such as the Mass and Daily Office, will be described in terms of not only their traditional texts,[19] but especially in terms of the devotional process they formalize. In understanding liturgical events in this way, we can more meaningfully relate musical style to its context. The question becomes not what musical style(s) is traditionally associated with particular liturgical texts, but rather

17. SL, 741.

18. Morris Berman. *Coming to Our Senses* (New York: Bantam Books, 1989), 116.

what liturgical process is active and how does a particular musical style function within that process. This "process" view seeks to replace a picture of liturgy as a static sequence of text-governed events with one that takes into account the flow of human dynamics encoded within those events...and to see music as an important agent in those dynamics. Again, the task is an interpretative one, necessarily so, as Avery Dulles underscores:

> Objective scientific knowledge is particularly unsuited to give intimate knowledge of living subjects, insofar as they are individual, free, and personal. Our strictly personal knowledge of other human beings must proceed by another route. It is achieved through interpretation of the signs—the words and gestures—by which people express themselves. By a kind of synthetic discernment, one can intuit the state of the soul which lies at the root of a certain set of manifestations, even though one cannot prove by formal argument the validity of the intuition. We rely on subtle techniques of interpretation.[20]

It is to that task that we now turn.

---

19. John Harper's recent *The Forms and Orders of Western Liturgy from the Tenth to the Eighteenth Century* (Oxford: Clarendon Press, 1991) is a valuable resource for the objective study of liturgy in a textual perspective. Moreover, aimed at a musical audience, its publication marks the growing interest in liturgical musicology.

20. Avery Dulles. "The Symbolic Structure of Revelation." *Theological Studies* 41 (1980): 51-73.

2

Time and Text

> *"As in the prism the rays of the one sun are broken up into different colors, so in the Church's year is the plentitude of the eternal divine sun broken up."*[1]

MANY have put forth the association of circularity with the sacred and the whole. The "rose window" of the Gothic cathedral or the ubiquitous halo as an iconic badge of sanctity are familiar and specifically Christian manifestations of a universal idea. Jungian thinkers have been quick to underscore the importance of the circle as well. Aniela Jaffé summarizes from the psychological point of view:

> [The circle or sphere] expresses the totality of the psyche in all its aspects, including the relationship between man and the whole of nature. Whether the symbol of the circle appears in primitive sun worship or modern religion, in myths or dreams, in the mandalas drawn by Tibetan monks, in the ground plans of cities, or in the spherical concepts of early astronomers, it always points to the single most vital aspect of life—its

1. Friedrich Heiler, "Contemplation in Christian Mysticism," in *Spiritual Disciplines: Papers from the Eranos Yearbooks* (Princeton: Princeton University Press, 1985), 209.

ultimate wholeness...In terms of psychological symbolism, it expresses the union of opposites—the union
of the personal, temporal world of the ego with the
non-personal, timeless world of the non-ego. Ultimately, this union is the fulfillment and goal of all religions:
It is the union of the soul with God.[2]

Ritual gestures and actions richly draw on this symbol. Psalm
26:6 proclaims

> I will wash my hands in innocence, O Lord,
> that I may go in procession round your altar,

suggesting a "ceremonial encircling dance" in the Old Testament world.[3] (Interestingly, the religious act of encircling in
dance was also associated with fertility, as Gerardus van der
Leeuw notes: "[T]he round dances (*rondes*) arose out of the
magic circle which the dancers described around a holy object,
tree, post, or well, and, on occasion, around the coveted woman or the coveted man, or around the field which is to yield the
crop.")[4] The Old Testament ceremonial encircling dance is
strikingly similar to the Christian "dance" of incensation—an
encircling of the altar by the celebrant with smoking thurible
(incense pot)—done at the beginning of Mass and at the Offertory. This echoes preliminary encirclings of the church itself. E.
O. James records: "In the medieval rite before approaching the
altar the sacred ministers with their attendants circumvented
the cathedral, following the course of the sun in the sky, except

2. Aniela Jaffé, "Symbolism in the Visual Arts," in *Man and
His Symbols* (New York: Dell Publishing, 1968), 266-268.

3. See W.O. E. Oesterley, "Worship in the Old Testament,"
in *Liturgy and Worship* (London: SPCK, 1954), 49.

4. Gerardus van der Leeuw, *Sacred and Profane Beauty: The
Holy in Art* (New York: Holt, Rinehart and Winston,
1963), 22.

on penitential occasions, when the direction was reversed." The reversal of direction in association with penitence is also noteworthy, as moving opposite the direction of the sun implies moving against time, into the past, where recollection and examination occur.[5]

The Gnostic "Acts of John" records a circle dance led by Jesus after the Last Supper of Maundy Thursday. Jesus says, "Before I am given over to them [the arresting Jews], let us sing a hymn to the Father, and thus go to meet what lies ahead." The account continues

> So he bade us form a circle, as it were, holding each other's hands, and taking his place in the middle he said: 'Answer Amen to me.' Then he began to hymn and to say: 'Glory be to the Father.' And we, forming a circle, responded 'Amen' to him.[6]

Jung's comments in this context are well targeted: "[T]he aim and effect of the solemn round dance is to impress upon the mind the image of the circle and the centre and the relation of each point along the periphery to that centre. Psychologically this arrangement is equivalent to a mandala and is thus a symbol of the self...."[7]

Circularity finds one of its strongest manifestations in our perception of time. Secular time proceeds linearly, a progression towards a goal from a goal. Sacred time, on the other hand, is like the eternal revolution of a wheel, a cyclical process in which the past returns as the present, and this "eternal return" is especially marked by ritual or even ushered in by rit-

5. E. O. James, Christian *Myth and Ritual: A Historical Study* (1933; Cleveland: World Publishing, 1965), 146.

6. MELC, 25.

ual. Mircea Eliade, in classic studies of humankind's religious behavior notes that "sacred time is indefinitely recoverable, indefinitely repeatable…it always remains equal to itself, it neither changes nor is exhausted…It can be said of sacred time that it is always the same, that it is 'a succession of eternities'."[8] The "return" is in the nature of sacred time; in this sense we do not cause it. However, it is *through* ritual action, liturgical observance, that its circular nature transcends our linear, historical temporality.

The associations of circularity, sacred time, and music are close knit, and go beyond the liturgical repetition of chants within the cycle of the year or the repetition forms they sometimes embrace. In some instances the music, in response perhaps to its liturgical aura, becomes gesturally circular. For example, Cristobal Morales' motet *Emendemus in melius* dramatically juxtaposes two Ash Wednesday texts: four voices sing "Emendemus in melius":

> Let us amend for the better those things in which we have sinned through ignorance…Attend, O Lord, and have mercy: for we have sinned against you.

Another voice sings "memento homo quia pulvis es":

7. See Jung, "Transformation Symbols," 172. Mandala images appear in several contexts within the Western spiritual tradition. Striking examples may be found in the illuminations which accompany Hildegard of Bingen's visionary *Scivias* (1141-1151). For a modern edition, see Hildegard of Bingen, *Scivias*, trans. Columba Hart and Jane Bishop (Mahwah, N.J.: The Paulist Press, 1990). For a poetic example of mandala imagery, see Canto xxxiii from Dante's *Il Paradiso.*

8. Eliade, *Sacred and Profane* 69, 88. See also his *Cosmos and History: the Myth of the Eternal Return* (New York: Harper Torchbooks, 1959).

> Remember, man, that you are dust and unto dust shall
> you return.

The second text is set to an ostinato figure, cyclically confront-
ing the anxious sinner (of the first text) with its *memento mori*.
The confrontation is thus inescapable (as death is inescapable),
timeless (as death is universal), and, in its renunciation of linear
time, "sacred." Similar in effect and situation is Heinrich Isaac's
Quis dabit capiti meo aquam, a lament on the death of Lorenzo
de Medici in 1492 with a text by the humanist Poliziano. The
third stanza, marked "Laurus [Lorenzo] tacet" appropriately re-
duces the four-voice texture to three voices, the lowest of which
cyclically repeats "requiescamus in pace" [and may we rest in
peace]. Its repetition forms an ostinato—again timeless, repeatable, inescapable, universal, and sacred—with the added drama
of each repetition dropping a scale step lower…closer to the
grave. (One may argue that I confuse the "timeless" and the "inescapable" with the "sacred" here, and must along these lines
also see Dido's lament in Purcell's *Dido and Aeneas* as a "sacred"
moment. It is important to stress that the confrontation with
death *in whatever context* elicits a certain sacrality. However, the
liturgical texts and intention of Morales' motet and the liturgical quotation in Isaac's lament provide a context that clearly in-
forms our perception of their circularity… and sacrality.)

Other examples forego ostinato but seem to renounce linear goals to a similar end. Bach's "Herr, unser Herrscher," the
opening movement of the *St. John Passion*, for instance,
strongly evokes restlessness, disquietude, and a sense of
impending tragedy. These affective impressions derive from
the lengthy tonic pedal point, the seemingly unceasing sighs of
the violas, the hovering narrow intervals of the violins, and the
large number of close suspensions in the woodwinds. There is
lots of motion, but it is unchanging; it seems to have already
begun before the first measure (cf. Eliade: "it always remains
equal to itself; it neither changes nor is exhausted.") Its goals,
though not absent[9] are a long time in forming. The pedal

point obscures harmonic teleology, and when the pedal ceases, it is replaced by sequence around the circle of fifths. The sequence is *syntactically* goal oriented, as dominants "require" their tonics in succession, but in a larger sense there seems no goal at all, as the sequence could be perpetuated *ad infinitum.* In short, what Bach seems to be doing here is moving us into the aural world of unchanging circles—a sacred wheel; *the* sacred wheel whose rotation unfolds the events of the Passion.

The phenomenon of circularity is formalized in the liturgy's organization of the year and the day. And the year and day is so organized in order that it may be consecrated. Human existence, bound in time, in seeking the timeless must nevertheless own its temporality. Louis Bouyer writes:

> Our created nature is so bound up with this created time in which all living beings live that our being cannot be taken up into the divine unless the time which is connatural to us is also in some way taken up.[10]

One way in which it is "taken up" is in the creation of annual and diurnal cycles. The church year exists as the turning of two concentric wheels, within which wheels of various smaller sizes also turn.

The Large Cycles: the Temporale and the Sanctorale

One cycle is the *Temporale,* a seasonal movement including all Sundays, centering on the life of Jesus. Within this large cycle, two smaller wheels turn: the Christmas Cycle and the Easter Cycle, a scheme in place since 400.

9. See, for example, the strong harmonic preparation of the initial choral entry (mm. 16-19).

10. Bouyer, *Liturgical Piety* 194.

I. CHRISTMAS CYCLE

ADVENT — A penitential season encompassing the four Sundays preceding Christmas. Traditional themes include the Last Judgement and Second Coming of Christ, the ministry of John the Baptist as a prophetic forerunner of Jesus as Messiah, and the Triumphal Entry of Jesus into Jerusalem. The emphasis is on the *coming* of the Messiah and the attendant preparation for the event.

CHRISTMAS — The celebration of Jesus' birth, observed on Dec. 25 since the fourth century (a Christian replacement of the pagan "Birthday of the Invincible Sun"). The celebration extends throughout "Christmastide" until January 6, including commemorations of associated events like the "Slaughter of the Innocents" (Dec. 28) and the Circumcision (Jan. 1).

EPIPHANY — A season of variable length beginning on January 6 devoted to the manifestations of Jesus as the Christ. Texts focus on the visit of the Three Magi to Bethlehem, the twelve-year-old Jesus among the teachers in the Temple, his first miracle of changing water into wine at a wedding in Cana, miraculous healings by his hand, and the miraculous quieting of a storm on the Sea of Galilee.

The season—and the cycle—historically ended with "pre-Lent": the Sundays Septuagesima, Sexagesima, and Quinquagesima.

II. EASTER CYCLE

LENT — A penitential season encompassing Ash Wednesday (so-called because ashes are imposed on the foreheads of the community as a sign of penitence and mortification), five Sundays following, and Holy Week. The period of penitential preparation before a celebration (here, Easter) seems a natural sequence, and Christians crafted an analogy between their 40 days of mortification (the Lenten period, less Sundays) and Jesus' 40 days of temptation in the wilderness prior to beginning his ministry. However, this is a later development. Prior to the fourth century, this period was a highly disciplined time of preparation for catechumens who were to be baptized at Easter. It is their pre-Baptismal rigor that becomes the model for the pre-Easter preparation of the whole community. Holy Week, the final week of the season, focuses on the events leading up to Jesus' crucifixion:

(a) Triumphal entry into Jerusalem and Jesus' Passion — Palm Sunday

(b) Institution of the Eucharist at the Last Supper — Maundy Thursday

(c) Jesus' Passion — Good Friday

(Maundy Thursday, Good Friday, and Holy Saturday—the last three days of Holy Week are known collectively as the *Triduum Sacrum*.)

PASCHAL TIME (Eastertide) — 50-day celebration of the resurrection   of Jesus, ushered in on Easter Sunday. Easter was also the traditional time for baptism (cf. preparation, above) as in baptism one dies to sin and is born to new life, analogous to Jesus' death and resurrection. On the fifth Thursday after Easter, the Church focuses on Christ's Ascension into heaven, the end of his bodily presence one earth, 40 days after Easter, leaving the Apostles with the promise that the Holy Spirit would come among them.

PENTECOST — A lengthy season of variable length (up to over twenty-five Sundays). ushered in by Pentecost Sunday (Whitsunday) on which the Church celebrates the descent of the Holy Spirit and, in essence, its beginnings as a church. The season of Pentecost completes the Easter cycle and the cycle of the *Temporale*.

The *Sanctorale* cycle "turns" at the same time as the *Temporale*, focusing not on the life of Jesus, but rather on the lives of saints of the church. Canonized saints have their own feast day assigned on the calendar—August 31 for Aidan, July 11 for Benedict, etc.

The calendar is hierarchical. For example, when the *Temporale* and *Sanctorale* come into conflict—as inevitably they do— rules of precedence transfer one occasion to another day. Also, hierarchical organization inflects certain days as more "important" than others, requiring more elaborate ceremonial. The degree of ceremonial elaboration is just one factor in giving liturgical times distinct flavors. Liturgical seasons are marked by distinctive colors, and the color is found as the prominent hue in the vestments and sanctuary, although the color scheme—purple for penitential Advent and Lent, green for Epiphany, white for Easter, etc.—is not firmly codified until the nineteenth century. Sound too is significant. Periods of mourning and penance would see the silencing of musical instruments; bells would be replaced by wooden clapboards, etc. Texts are omitted in regard of the mood of the season, as well. Penitential Lent "buries" the praiseful "Alleluia," not to be heard until it is "resurrected" at Easter, and so too the "Gloria in excelsis Deo." Similarly, the importance of a day in the calendar elicits certain degrees of musical elaboration. In the Middle Ages this could take several shapes. Adding melismas,

new texts, or new text and music to a given chant, troping, for
instance, was one way of inflecting the particularity and the
importance of a given day. Troping could be vertical as well as
horizontal, as polyphony—in a sense, a vertical trope of a
chant—set a day apart from the more accustomed monophonic chant of the liturgy. One of the more colorful documenta-
tions of this is the papal bull *Docta Sanctorum Patrum* (1324-
25) of Pope John XXII.   The bull, written amid the blossom-
ing *Ars Nova*, is strongly critical and proscriptive of contemporary polyphonic style, featuring often rigorous rhythmic
complexity with an admixture of the vernacular. Yet even in
such a conservative, critical document, the pope preserves
polyphony as ornament for special occasions:

> However, We do not intend to forbid the occasional
> use—*principally on solemn feasts at Mass and at Divine
> Office* [emphasis added]—of certain consonant inter-
> vals   superposed   upon   the   simple   ecclesiastical
> chant…for such consonances are pleasing to the ear
> and arouse devotion, and they prevent torpor among
> those who sing in honor of God.[11]

Similarly, the rich organal school of Notre Dame in Paris was
hierarchical in its use of polyphony as an inflection of the liturgical calendar: only certain feasts utilized organa, and the extent
to which they were used was tied to the rank of the feast.[12] Although polyphony is clearly more complex than monophonic
chant, i.e. it exists in more dimensions, its use as ornamenta-

---

11. See Robert F. Hayburn, *Papal Legislation on Sacred
Music 95 A.D. to 1977 A.D.* (Collegeville, Minn.: The
Liturgical Press,1979), 21.

12. See Craig Wright, *Music and Ceremony at Notre Dame,
500-1500* (Cambridge: Cambridge University Press, 1989),
265-266.

tion perhaps owes as much or more to its "outsider" status as to its intrinsic quality. For example, in our own day, where plainchant has become the "outsider," we see that it is chant—archaic and "other"—that tends to grace solemn occasions as ornament.

The "wheels within wheels" scheme that we perceive in, for example, the Easter and Christmas cycles within the *Temporale* are echoed at yet other levels. Most familiar is the weekly cycle with its special attention given to Sunday as the Lord's Day, not in an attempt to create a Christian sabbath along Hebrew lines, but in honor of the day of the resurrection. And the day itself was soon enough a round of prayer, following the Hebrew model of prayer at particular times of day. The *Didache* (first century) specifies prayer three times a day; Tertullian (d. post 220) specifies the third, sixth, and ninth hours (9:00, 12:00, and 3:00), acknowledging common divisions of the day;[13] the *Apostolic Tradition* of Hippolytus (c. 215) relates these hours to Jesus' passion on the cross on Good Friday. Tertullian and Hippolytus both expect morning and evening prayer as well.[14] Early monastics (fourth and fifth century) held to an ideal of unceasing prayer—an unsurprising aspect of their zeal—though they would meet in common several times a day for corporate prayer: in Egypt twice a day, in Palestine, six.[15] Both expectations surface in the following story from the Desert Fathers:

> Epiphanius, of holy memory, the bishop from Cyprus,. was told this by the abbot of his monastery in Palestine.

13. See Robert Taft, SJ, *The Liturgy of the Hours* (Collegeville, Minn.: The Liturgical Press, 1986), 8-19.

14. Jungmann, *Christian Prayer*, 8-10.

15. See E. C. Ratcliff, "The Choir Offices," in *Liturgy and Worship* (London: SPCK, 1954), 260. See also Dix, 326.

'By your prayers we have kept our rule; we carefully observe the offices of terce sext, none [3rd, 6th, and 9th
hours] and vespers.' But Epiphanius rebuked him and
said: 'Then you are surely failing to pray at other times.
The true monk ought to pray without ceasing, ought
always to be singing psalms in his heart.'[16]

A seven-fold round of daily offices, echoing Ps. 119. v. 164
("Seven times a day do I praise you") is described by John Cassian in his fifth-century. *Institutes of the Coenobites*. Cassian
writes of his experience as a monk at Bethlehem, but significantly, a similar course of offices for the secular, i.e. non-monas-
tic, church is in place in Jerusalem in the 4th cent., attested to
by the Spanish pilgrim Egeria in 385. All times of day are now
being sanctified by corporate prayer, and though the monastic
ideal of unceasing prayer was perhaps attainable by those who
vocationally could give themselves to it, those in the world, as
evidenced by Egeria, could respond to the same urge by following a daily round of offices.

The daily office is given shape, long life, and wide dissemi-
nation as it is embodied in the *Rule of St. Benedict* (d. ca. 547).
Benedict's rule—his authorship is currently questioned—
guides the monastic community with a "fund of spiritual and
human wisdom" for "all the vicissitudes of life"[17] as they
might have been encountered by those living under his direction at Monte Cassino in the sixth century. It became and
remains, however, a central expression of Western monasticism
to our own day. Of the office, he writes:

16. "Sayings of the Fathers," in *Western Asceticism*, ed.
Owen Chadwick (Philadelphia: The Westminster Press,
1958), 142.

17. David Knowles, *Christian Monasticism* (New York:
World University Press, 1969), 34.

Seven times a day have I praised thee,' said the prophet.
We shall perform this consecrated number of seven if
we offer prayer (the duty of our profession) at the hours
of Lauds, Prime, Terce, Sext, None, Vespers, and Compline. It was of these day hours that he [the prophet/
psalmist] said: 'Seven times a day have I praised thee.'
Elsewhere the same prophet makes mention of the
night office, 'at midnight I rose to confess to thee.' At
these times, therefore, let us render praise to our creator
'for the judgement of his justice'—that is, Lauds,
Prime, Terce, Sext, None, Vespers, Compline, and let
us rise at night to confess him.[18]

Thus an eight-fold scheme is standardized following the temporal references of Ps. 119, as illustrated below:

THE DIVINE OFFICE

Matins — 2 a.m.

   The night office, recalling vigils of the early church

Lauds — Daybreak

   So-called because of the recurrence of the word
   "Laudate" in its associated psalmody (Pss. 148-
   150).

Prime — 6 a.m. (First hour of the day)

Terce — 9 a.m. (Third hour of the day)

Sext — 12 p.m. (Sixth hour of the day)

None — 3 p.m. (Ninth hour of the day)

18. "The Rule of Saint Benedict," in *Western Asceticism*,
307.

Vespers — Last hour of daylight

Compline — Before retiring (to "complete" the day)

The schedule, though not continuous, did offer up all of the various parts of the day—early morning, midday, afternoon, early evening, etc.—and in so doing, the passing of time itself prompts spiritual introspection, as Friedrich Heiler observes:

> Side by side with the spatial, earthly, and corporeal symbols stand the holy hours as stimuli to and object of meditation. In the Church's prayers for the "hours," the natural course of the day becomes a plan of meditation. The daily hymns of the Latin Breviary make the sun's passage into a symbol of the most fervent relations between the soul and God. By night, at Matins, the congregation waits with yearning for the coming light; in early morning, at Lauds, it sings the praise of the dawning light; at Prime (6 a.m.), it humbly worships the rising spiritual sun, Jesus Christ; at Tierce (9 a.m.), it contemplates the growing light; at Sext (noon), its climax; at None (3 p.m.), the waning light; at Vespers, the dawning of the eternal light as the earthly light departs.[19]

The rhythms of the natural day, especially as they involve light and dark, are strongly present in office hymns—as metaphors of spiritual light and darkness, to be sure, but moreover as a way of lifting up the mundane to consecration. Many Office hymns demonstrate this point. The following Matins texts, sung in the pre-dawn morning, refer to awaking from sleep, and they look to morning to chase night away as divine light chases away sin.

19. Heiler, "Contemplation in Christian Mysticism," 208-209.

Somno refectis artubus[20]

1. Our limbs refresh'd with slumber now,
    And sloth cast off, in prayer we bow;
    And while we sing thy praises dear,
    O Father, be thou present here!

2. To thee our earliest morning song
    To thee our heart's full powers belong
    And thou, O Holy One, prevent
    Each following action and intent

3. As shades at morning flee away,
    And night before the star of day,
    So each transgression of the night
    Be purged by thee, celestial Light.

Consors paterni luminis

1. Thou sharer of the Father's Light
    Thou very Light of light and day,
    The night is broken by our songs;
    Look on thy suppliants as we pray.

2. Scatter the darkness of our hearts,
    Drive back the armies of our foes;
    Let us not yield to slothful ease,
    Nor let soft sleep our eyelids close.

Rerum Creator optime

1. Creator Blest, thy servant's Guide,
    Hear us who in thy help confide,
    To set us free from sinful rest,
    And slumber which thou hast not blest.

---

20. Hymn translations here and below are from *The Divine Office*, 2 vols. (London: Geoffrey Cumberlege, 1953).

Nox atra rerum contegit

1. All things of earth most fair and bright
    Lie hid beneath night's dreamy veil;
    O righteous Judge of human hearts,
    Now let our lowly prayers avail.

2. Put now away our grievous sins,
    Upon our darkness cast thy light;
    And by thy blessed grace, good Lord,
    Save us from sin, and from its might.

4. Drive backward then the shades of night
    The deepest shades, within that lie;
    And lift thy servants to the Light
    That glows for all eternity.

Lauds is sung at dawn, a symbolically rich juncture, as dawn recalls Peter's denial of Jesus,[21] suggests "enlightenment," and, as
forerunner of day, reminds of Jesus' coming.

Aeterne rerum Conditor

5. Arise ye then, with one accord;
    No longer wrapt in slumber lie;
    The cock rebukes all who their Lord
    By sloth neglect, by sin deny.

8. Awake us from false sleep profound,
    And through our senses pour thy light:
    Be thy blest Name, the first we sound
    At early dawn, the last at night.

---

21. "One of the servants of the high priest…asked, 'Did I
not see you in the garden with him [Jesus]?' Again Peter
denied it, and at that moment the cock crowed." John 18:
26-27.

Splendor paternae gloriae

1. Thou brightness of the Father's ray
   True Light of light, and Day of day;
   Light's fountain and eternal Spring;
   Thou Morn, the morn illumining.

2. Glide in, thou very Sun divine;
   With everlasting brightness shine;
   And shed abroad on every sense
   The Spirit's light and influence.

Ales diei nuntius

1. The winged herald of the day
   Proclaims the morn's approaching ray:
   And Christ the Lord our souls excites,
   And so to endless Life invites

Nox et tenebrae

1. Hence, night and clouds that night-time brings,
   Confus'd and dark and troubled things;
   The dawn is here; the sky grows white;
   Christ is at hand; depart from sight![22]

None, sung in the afternoon, looks toward evening and invites the comparison of night's rest and eternal rest.

22. The association of Christ with the sun is echoed in the practice of facing east in prayer, as recorded by Clement of Rome, Origen, and Tertullian. See Taft, *The Liturgy of the Hours*, 28. As a visual image it is particularly evident in ray-bedecked monstrances of the Baroque era.

Rerum Deus tenax vigor

2. Grant us, when this short life is past,
    The glorious evening that shall last;
    That by a holy death attain'd,
    Eternal glory may be gain'd.

Vespers too is specific in reference to night coming and its attendant fears.

Lucis Creator optime

1. O Blest Creator of the Light,
    Who mak'st the day with radiance bright,
    And o'er the forming world didst call
    The light from chaos first of all;

2. Whose wisdom joined in meet array
    The morn and eve, and named them day;
    Night comes with all its darkling fears,
    Regard thy people's prayers and tears.

O Lux beata Trinitas

1. O Trinity of blessed light,
    O Unity of princely might,
    The fiery sun now goes his way;
    Shed thou within our hearts thy ray.

Compline bids God watch over sleep.

Te lucis ante terminum

1. Before the ending of the day,
    Creator of the world se pray
    That with thy wonted favour thou
    Woulds't be our Guard and Keeper now.

We observe in the sum of these examples the richness of the natural rhythms of the day, both in and of themselves and as evocations of God's presence in the dimension of time. As symbolic vectors pointing to the divine, they shape and give form to the liturgical *rota*, the offering up of all parts of the day in praise, a blessing of the mundane.

Thus far our discussion of time has focussed on a few basic ideas: the holiness/wholeness of circularity and its temporal manifestations in the liturgical year, week, and day. The temporal dimensions of liturgy, however, transcend these rational aspects of calendar; experientially liturgy invites one to live beyond time as well. We see this in several ways. One has to do with the simultaneity of earthly and heavenly liturgy; what takes place in the church on earth is a coincident echo of that which takes place in heaven, as John Chrysostom describes:

> Above, the hosts of angels sing praise; below, men form choirs in the churches and imitate them by singing the same doxology, Above, the seraphim cry out in the Tersanctus; below, the human throng sends up the same cry. The inhabitants of heaven and earth are brought together in a common solemn assembly; there is one thanksgiving, one shout of delight, one joyful chorus.[23]

Yet the inhabitants of heaven exist beyond what we know as historical time. Liturgy then offers a bridge between the dimensions... the timeless breaks into time; time is lifted up into the timeless. Similarly too the rendition of parts of the liturgy—its manner of performance—underscores the breakdown of rational time. For example, as we will discuss at greater length in the chapter devoted to the mass, certain texts of the mass overlap in performance, obscuring rational linearity and rational comprehension of the texts. In this light, the relationship of the

---

23. "Homilia I in Oziam sen de Seraphinis" MECL, 89.

choral acclamation of "Sanctus" and the prayer of consecration is a telling case in point. From the standpoint of text, the Sanctus is *to be followed* by prayers said by the priest at the altar. Traditionally, however, the priest says the prayers in a low voice *during* the Sanctus. This simultaneity is significant. If the wall of time separating earth and heaven has been ritually broken, the Sanctus—sung unceasingly by the angelic choir in heaven—will naturally persist "unceasingly" amid the linear earthly prayer of the priest. The simultaneous performance evokes the mystical bridging of linear and non-linear time. The bridge is never more apparent than in the mysterious temporality of Christ's historical sacrifice which, following Roman theology, is ritually made present in each mass. Christ's sacrifice in historical time and place is not "remembered" or "memorialized" as much as it is "presently operative by its effects."[24] The sacrifice was historical, a past-tense event, but through ritual action it enjoys an eternal present tense.

The church's various ways of organizing time move in the direction of formality; similarly, the church's approach to text. The early church's liturgy, judging from the *First Apology of Justin Martyr* (c. 155) preserved extemporaneous elements, even, or especially, in the heart of the eucharist:

> When the reader has finished, the president [bishop] in a discourse, admonishes and invites the people to practice these examples of virtue. Then we all stand up together and offer prayers. And...when we have finished the prayer, bread is presented, and wine with water; the president likewise offers up prayers and thanksgivings

24. SL, 245.

according to his ability [emphasis added], and the people assent by saying, Amen.[25]

With the fifth century, the celebrant prayed not "according to his ability," but generally according to fixed texts.[26] By the time of Charlemagne the performance of the Divine Office required at least 10 books for the participants needing scripture, prayers, chants, and ceremonial prescription at hand.[27]

Liturgical texts are of two kinds: the Proper and the Ordinary. The texts of the Ordinary are those that are used on all occasions of like kind, for example texts that are common to all masses, or all Vespers. However, the texts of the Proper are specific to a given occasion, only, for instance, the Mass of St. Stephen or Vespers for the Dead. The development of the Proper takes place gradually over a long period of time. As detailed by Dom Gregory Dix, a nucleus of the Proper is in place by the end of the fifth century, including Paschal lessons (the oldest layer), Holy Saturday, some of the seasons—Christ-

25. Cited in *Liturgies of the Western Church*, ed. by Bard Thompson (Philadelpia: Fortress Press, 1961), 9.

26. See D.M. Hope, "Medieval Western Rites" in *The Study of Liturgy* (New York: Oxford University Press, 1992), 267. The *Apostolic Tradition* of Hippolytus (c. 220) is in a sense a watershed. As Theodor Klauser notes, it was "the first book to supply not merely the main themes of the prayer to be improvised upon, but rather a pattern of fixed prayer formulas for the liturgy." *A Short History of the Western Liturgy* (1965; Eng. trans., Oxford: Oxford University Press, 1979), 12. For Hippolytus' text, see *Liturgies of the Western Church*, 13-24. The origins, authorship, and original reading of the *Apostolic Tradition* are uncertain. For a recent discussion, see Paul Bradshaw, *The Search for the Origins of Christian Worship* (New York: Oxford University Press, 1992).

27. W. Jardine Grisbrooke, "The Formative Period Cathedral and Monastic Offices," in *The Study of Liturgy*, 425.

mas, Lent, Easter—and some of the lesser martyrs. By the end of the sixth century, Advent, Pre-Lent, and the five Sundays of Eastertide are in place. The rest of the Sunday Proper was slow to develop.[28] The slowness of the development and the degree of variability it requires (having much to do with regional as well as chronological concerns) is significant, for although the texts seek, in part, to fix and control the liturgical action—to objectify it—they do so ideally in tension with subjective elements. As Louis Bouyer tellingly observes: "The authority attached to the liturgy was...fundamentally that of tradition itself. And it was only as the guarantor of tradition under both its aspects of permanence [text] and of living adaptability that the authority of Popes and Bishops gave their sanction to the liturgy."[29]

The degree of fixity and control in the liturgy—set prayers, lessons, and ceremonial procedures—invites further comment, even in an introductory context, as here. There are a number of reasons why liturgy became so "fixed."

(1) *Uniformity as a measure of catholicity.* Fixed texts promoted uniform practice, a strongly visible symbol of the church's claim to universality or catholicity. In essence, one truth, one practice. This could have political ramifications as well. For example, liturgical uniformity received considerable attention by the Carolingians, under whose leadership the Frankish kingdom adopted the Roman rite, an action related to Pepin's need for papal confirmation of his claim to the throne. Here, as in other historical contexts, liturgical uniformity also manifested political unity: as local power bent the knee to one king, so too did diverse local church practices accede to one rite.[30]

---

28. Following SL, 363-64.

29. Bouyer, *Liturgical Piety*, 71-72.

(2) *Ritual repetition requires fixity.* The Trappist monk Thomas Merton, in *The New Man* points to humankind's ability to signify the holy with words:

> Words, names, and signs...will flower into many kinds of creative intellectual activity. They will become, first of all, poems which will express man's inexpressible intuitions of hidden reality of created things. They will become philosophy and science...Finally words will become *sacred* signs. They will acquire the power to set apart certain elements of creation and make them holy.[31]

And that which is set apart becomes ritualized by repetition. Moreover, the fixity not only enables the text to be repeated, but also promotes a linkage with the historical time of Jesus in an objective sense as it is objectively his words at the Last Supper that are ritually repeated in the canon of the mass.

(3) *Control as a measure of orthodoxy.* Fixed texts impeded idiosyncratic or heretical interpretations of the liturgy by an individual or a group. In much the same way as the early church enacted its mysteries protectively behind closed doors, the textual "closed door" protected against the taint of unorthodoxy. In a similar way, too, the fixed text relieved liturgical leaders lacking education and/or charism from a taint of a different kind ...the taint of an inability to improvise the prayers successfully.[32]

---

30. Cf. Wright, *Music and Ceremony at Notre Dame*, 61.

31. Thomas Merton, *The New Man* (1961; New York: Bantam Books, 1981), 49.

32. See Klauser, *Short History*, 12.

(4) *Fixity as craftsmanship.* In compiling a fixed text, the liturgy's "dance" became "choreographed" in finely crafted ways. Texts were generally[33] interwoven with seasonal themes or were chosen with an eye toward their function (introits with texts of movement; "O Taste and See" at the Communion, etc.). Texts were also selected with an eye toward their interaction, as Ruth Steiner observes with regard to Matins responsories, noting that their texts invite reflective meditation on the lesson they follow.[34]

These several reasons for a canonical liturgical text touch foundational issues of catholicity and ritual behavior. The fixity of liturgical text, however, is always in tension with authenticity of participation. The two ideally coexist with the fixed text a fluid vehicle for the authentic participation of the individual or the community, neither precluding the other. Historically the balance between the two has often been shy of this ideal, and liturgy has become at various times "the text" and not the action through the text. Modern comment is well focussed and clear in its intent on this issue. The contrast of liturgy as something done, not something said (or seen) is much a part of Dom Gregory's classic study, which sees the eucharist as a shape formed by four *actions*.[35] Similarly, Louis Bouyer attacks the false concept of liturgy seen as "compulsory

---

33. Generally, but not always. Bouyer underscores the capacity of liturgical texts to exist "out of time" as well: "It is remarkable nevertheless that even today the Liturgy of the Lord's Supper is suffused with the proclamation of His final glory; the worship of the Cross on Good Friday resounds with shouts of victory; and, on Easter Sunday, the exultation in the Resurrection expresses itself in the words [from the Easter sequence "Victimae paschali laudes]:…" Death and life fought in a marvelous struggle." See *Liturgical Piety*, Piety, 191.

34. Ruth Steiner. "The Music for a Cluny Office of St. Benedict." in *Monasticism and the Arts*, 82.

ceremonial, the rule for external manifestations of worship."
He traces this view to the "operatic" seventeenth century, and
his contemporary witnesses to the norm of passive participation are telling. For example, the saintly and sainted Francis de
Sales, presumably a model of piety, made "a sort of pious resolution always to say his beads when his [episcopal] duties
required him to attend a public mass."[36] In other words, even
those especially given to liturgical life chose to participate not
in the action of the liturgy, but rather in a collateral, private
act rendered in the aura of the liturgy.

Much earlier (in monasteries by the eighth century), the
advent of the private mass, a ceremony rendered by a priest
and his server, reduced *community* action to *individual*
act…the "priest's mass." Similarly, the liturgical text was priva-
tized during *public* mass with the priest's prayers whispered at
the altar. Even passively, one did not share in the text, for it
was safely enclosed in inaudibility. The whispered canon arose
in the West as early as the eighth century, in Rome by 1000.[37]
Although it radically altered the nature of the liturgical action,
it at the same time enhanced the mystery and awe of the pro-
ceedings: the words were whispered for they were "too holy to
say aloud." Emphasizing the privatization also is the subse-
quent relocation of the priest at the altar. Whereas earlier the
priest would celebrate behind the altar, in view of the community, now he would stand in front of the altar with his back to
the congregation, his body shielding the mystery from view.
Liturgical action is not only unheard; in this case, it is unseen
as well.[38]

---

35. SL, passim, esp. 12-15, 48.

36. Bouyer, *Liturgical Piety*, 2.

37. Klauser, *Short History*, 99.

Again, it is difficult to assess the authenticity of participation—it is a highly variable entity—though at times it is clear that the fixity and privatization of the text *allowed* the liturgy to focus on texted externals. For example, monastic liturgy after Benedict greatly increased in its complexity (and texting) culminating in the liturgy at eleventh-century Cluny where normal practice found a monk in corporate worship for more than eight hours a day; each monk would recite in the course of a day 215 psalms.[39] (Complexity of the text and rules were, of course, not unique to Cluny or even monasticism. In the sixteenth century, Thomas Cranmer on the complexity of the breviary observed: "Moreover, the number and hardness of the Rules called the *Pie*, and the manifold changings of the service, was the cause, that to turn the Book only was so hard and intricate a matter, that many times there was more business to find out what should be read, than to read it when it was found out.")[40]

Some of the elaboration here relates to the monks worshipping God on behalf of their secular peers. Of the relationship between benefactor and monastery Jungmann observes:

> The return on the part of the monastery took the form of a vastly augmented and unbroken recitation of the psalms by groups of monks who relieved each other in

38. Architecturally the choir screen also shielded the sanctuary and its action from public view.

39. See Jungmann, 85 and Knowles, 52. For discussion of the Cluniac day, see Noreen Hunt, *Cluny Under Saint Hugh 1049-1109* (London: Edward Arnold, 1967), 99-109, and Joan Evans *Monastic Life at Cluny 910-1157* (London: Oxford University Press, 1931), 78-97.

40. See Grisbrooke, "The Formative Period," 432.

turn at a work redounding, it is true, to God's honor but at the same time having in mind the spiritual welfare of founders and benefactors.[41]

The situation is strong comment on the degree to which liturgy could be nonparticipatory: at worst the text, at best the action, was something which only required saying or doing by *someone* to be efficacious. Individual participation in the action or the text was inessential. Indeed, some see it as a symptom of a contemporary lack of interiority. Charles Radding has provocatively put forth the idea that the world after Augustine (d. 430) until ca. 1050 witnesses the disappearance of interiority. He bases his thesis on concepts like the practice of simony (the selling of church offices), infant oblation (the practice of giving a child to the monastery without later confirming the child's interest in being there), and confession where penance and reparation could be done by another.[42] However, interiority may be seen to reemerge in the late Middle Ages in a number of ways, including pointed criticism of the above practices. With respect to the liturgy, Colin Morris has cited several new patterns of devotion which give witness to greater subjectivity, such as more hymns in the first-person, the rising of the cult of Mary, images of the crucifix replacing Christ in majesty, and kneeling for prayer.[43] Earlier eras explicitly owned their subjectivity. Cassian, writing on the monastic psalmody of the fourth century, observes:

41. Jungmann, *Christian Prayer*, 83.

42. See Charles Radding, *A World Made by Men: Cognition and Society, 400-1200* (Chapel Hill: University of North Carolina Press, 1985), passim, and Berman, *Coming to Our Senses*, 179-80. Cf. Caroline Walker Bynum, "Did the Twelfth Century Discover the Individual?" in *Jesus as Mother: Studies in the Spirituality of the High Middle Ages* (Berkeley: University of California Press, 1982).

They did not so much seem to be reciting the Psalms as to be re-creating them, for they said them from the heart as if they were extempore prayers.[44]

In considering liturgical text we have seen that through its fixity the liturgy becomes more an objective entity. And in this way it conforms to a large-scale Western trend that has increasingly promoted the objective and the visual over the subjective. Musical notation is an interesting example of this, where we see in Charlemagne's day only neumes of contour acting as memory aids; "exact" pitch recording appears first in the diastematic notation emerging around 1000.[45] Successive eras have gradually controlled more and more of the subjective musical event through written, visual means. A Renaissance

43. "Christian Civilization 1050-1400," in the *Oxford Illustrated History of Christianity* (Oxford: Oxford University Press, 1990), 218. Worldly manifestations would include the concept of romantic love and the beginning of the Crusades.

44. In Bouyer, *Liturgical Piety,* 229.

45. Significantly then, the reliance on musical memory maintains a strong subjective presence in the performance of liturgy long past the reliance on written texts. In a passage of considerable interest, Craig Wright links singing from memory and singing with a full heart on the basis of a common derivation from the word "corde." He remarks: "This verbal identity suggest that the true and pious manner of singing the praises of the Lord was one that involved a reaching within to a clear well spring from which would arise the sacred text and its medium of delivery. By implication then, singing from a book introduced an unnecessary impurity into the process." See Wright, *Music and Ceremony at Notre Dame,* 326.

motet will use exact pitch notation (though the pitches are sometimes performer inflected and do not necessarily imply a fixed pitch standard) and the rhythm will be precise. Things like scoring, expression, tempo, etc, are not indicated, but left to convention and performer discretion. A twentieth-century score, by contrast, will generally offer full instrumentation, detailed expression (not just "forte," but "fortississimo"), metronomic tempo indications, articulations, etc. The ascendancy of objectivity is clear here, and forms a musical echo to the increasing textual control of liturgical action.

In considering liturgical text, a second point to emerge is the tension between a fixed text and historical variability. Though liturgy deals with the timeless, its rendition is much conditioned by time and place. The fixity of the text precludes the intrusion of "continuing history" in the verbal canon, though these fixed elements become continuing factors against which historical change is measured, and through which history acts.

3

THE DAILY OFFICE

THE eight offices of the *diurnal* introduced in the previous chapter enjoy the familial similarity of siblings. They differ in degree of elaboration—Matins, Lauds, and Vespers have an expansiveness not found in the "lesser hours" of prime, terce, sext, and none—but they hold in common the elements of psalmody, scripture reading, prayer, and hymnody. The complex history of the divine office encompasses change in both specific detail as well as the very nature of the liturgy itself. For example, the elaborate ceremonial accretions of the later Middle Ages eventually yield place to more "streamlined" versions of the liturgy, as in Pope Innocent III's shortened office for his curia, adopted, revised, and widely disseminated by mendicant Franciscans. Later, in a striking transformation, the public, corporate forms of the office become private, clerical exercise. At the end of the sixteenth century, for instance, the Society of Jesus abandons the tradition of a choral office—the first order to do so—at which time it becomes a private, individual obligation for the Jesuits.[1] Earlier events presage this change, for the Counter-Reformation breakup of the monastic choral office may be seen to hearken back to the thirteenth century. At that

---

1. Other orders founded in the sixteenth century also rejected the obligation of the choral office. They include the Somaschi, the Clerks Regular of the Mother of God, the Camillians, and the Clerks Regular Minor. See Robert Taft, SJ, *The Liturgy of the Hours* (Collegeville, Minn.: The Liturgical Press, 1986), 302.

time, the travelling life of the new Mendicant orders constrained traditional practice. Living outside of a fixed community, as the begging life required, meant living away from
"choir"; accordingly, their office, following the curial breviary
of Innocent III, was non-corporate. Offered privately or in
choir, the Daily Office has been an enduring presence in the
spiritual life of the church. The daily recitation of the Office by
all priests, in choir or individually, was confirmed as recently as
Vatican II, at which time, however, the reduction of the lesser
hours in number from four to one and a slower course of
psalms eased the meeting of the obligation.[2]

The evolution of the office is too complex to pursue here.[3]
However, a look at its origins will allow us better to understand its enduring elements. W. Jardine Grisbrooke in writing
of the "formative period" of the office unravels the various
strands—essentially two—with which the fabric of the office is
woven.[4] The two strands are:

1. Non-eucharistic public worship of the secular church,
    the so-called "cathedral office," and
2. Monastic private devotion.

Interestingly, the intertwining of the two strands is particularly evident in the early and highly informative description

2. See *The Documents of Vatican II* (New York: The America Press, 1966), 164-5, # 89.

3. For discussion of the evolution of the office, see Pierre
Batiffol, *History of the Roman Breviary* (London: Longmans, Green, 1912); and more recently, *The Study of Liturgy*, 399-454, and Taft, *The Liturgy of the Hours*, passim.

4. See W. Jardine Grisbrooke, "The Formative Period—
Cathedral and Monastic Offices," in *The Study of Liturgy*
(1978; New York: Oxford University Press, 1992),403-
420., whose discussion I follow here. The identification of
the strands as "monastic" and "cathedral" is indebted to the
earlier work of Anton Baumstark.

of the fourth-century office in Jerusalem given by the Spanish pilgrim, Egeria.[5] Here the strands may be delineated by the participants' identity. As Grisbrooke reminds, "the daily offices in Jerusalem were of a hybrid character—partly public worship of the whole community, and partly the particular devotions of the monastic communities within it."[6] Thus the beginning of the morning and evening office found monks reciting the psalter like a "prelude" to the office proper—the monastic strand. Bishop and clergy would then enter and participate in a service given to prayer and blessing—the Cathedral office.[7] Historically it is the monastic elements of psalmodic recitation that become the most prominent strand in the fabric of the office, and this psalmodic recitation is an outgrowth of the monastic ideal of continuous personal prayer, a devotional practice of the individual that could at the same time be rendered corporately by the community. In other words, the psalmodic recitations were "aids to private meditative prayer to be practised in common."[8] The complete recita-

5. The *Itinerarium Egeriae* (?381-4) records the details of a three-year pilgrimage in the Holy Land. Liturgiologists have well noted her account of Holy Week in Jerusalem and its illuminating view of the catechumenal process. For an excerpt describing the daily liturgy in Jerusalem, see Taft, *Liturgy of the Hours*, 149. For a modern edition of Egeria's diary, see *Egeria: Diary of a Pilgrimage*, trans. George E. Gingras (New York: Newman Press, 1970).

6. Grisbrooke, "The Formative Period," 404.

7. The elements of the cathedral office, as described by Taft, *Liturgy of the Hours*, 47, include psalmody (Vulgate Psalm 62 in the morning, Psalm 140 at night); litanies for various groups of people, e.g. the catechumens, the penitents, and the faithful; collect; prayer of blessing; and dismissal. With regard to the psalmody of the cathedral office, it is important to note that it is selective as opposed to the numerically continuous cycle of the monastic office.

tion of the whole psalter, be it daily, weekly (as prescribed in the Rule of St. Benedict), or over a longer period of time has proven to be an enduring ideal.[9]

The psalmodic recitation forms the core of the office, as is made clear in the table below, a summary of the form for Sunday Vespers. Other offices feature similar construction.[10]

FORM FOR SUNDAY VESPERS

Opening Versicle and Response with Doxology

> a short, two-sentence dialogue with a short statement of praise to the Holy Trinity.

Four or Five Psalms with Antiphons

> Old Testament poetry—songs—with lyric refrains [antiphons], sometimes taken from the psalm itself, sometimes from other sources in reference to the Proper.

8. Grisbrooke, "The Formative Period," 405. On the lack of distinction between private and corporate prayer in early monasticism, see also Taft, *Liturgy of the Hours*, 66, 68, 71, and 364.

9. An ideal, but certainly not an unassailable one. The growth of the *Sanctorale* and the cultus of saints with its fewer proper psalms increasingly intruded on the *Temporale*'s course of full recitation. The effect was the repetition of selective psalms and the reduced use of the psalter *in toto*. The counteracting of this trend was a major point in the reform of the breviary in 1911 by Pope Pius X. See Batiffol, *Roman Breviary*, chap. 7, *passim*.

10. See, for example, the tabular summaries in Harper, *Forms and Orders*, 73-108. Chants for the office are presented in books entitled "Antiphonale." For the pre-Vatican II Roman Rite Office (monastic), see, for example, *Antiphonale Monasticum pro Diurnis Horis* ...(Paris, 1934).

The Little Chapter

> A very short scriptural passage

Brief Responsory

> A short, lyrical dialogue

Hymn

> Non-scriptural, strophic poetry

Versicle and Response

Canticle: Magnificat with antiphon

> Scriptural song, not from the Book of Psalms. (here the song of Mary sung in response to her cousin Elizabeth's recognition that Mary would be the mother of Jesus)

Kyrie eleison

Lord's Prayer

Collect

> A short prayer

Commemoration of the Sunday (at other times Suffrage of the Saints or Commemoration of the Cross)

> Antiphon, versicle and response, collect

Concluding versicles and responses.

Richard Crocker has recently contrasted the Mass and the Office from the standpoint of ritual action. He writes:

The underlying difference [between them] is that the
Mass is essentially a ritual act, while the office is a collection of texts to be said or sung. The Mass, of course,
includes many texts to be said or sung, but these function as accompaniment or explanation of the action,
whereas in the Office there is no action other than the
texts themselves.[11]

In a sense then, the office text locates an "action" in itself. The
ceremonial of Vespers, which can be elaborately solemn with
such things as censing of the altar(s) during the Magnificat,
finds ritual action secondary to recitation or, rather underscores
the recitation *as* the action. And in recalling the origins of the
psalmodic portion in the devotional practice of the early ascetic
monks, we are led to associate the psalmodic recitation with
their contemplative prayer.

Other traditions provocatively illumine the "activity" and
"wholeness" of recitation, as well as its mystical potential. In
the Hasidic tales associated with the Baal Shem Tov, for
instance, we find an account of the master and his scribe held
captive by pirates and the master's "secret knowledge" similarly
imprisoned in loss of memory. The scribe despairingly con-
fesses that he too has forgotten all…except his alphabet. At the
insistence of the Baal Shem Tov, the scribe begins to recite "the
sacred letters which contain all the mysteries of the entire uni-
verse." The master imitatively joins in the recitation until he
enters an ecstatic trance.   And it is from within the trance that
he breaks the curse.[12]

Psalmody in general admits a wide range of practice, styles,
functions, and attitudes. In context of the office, the psalms
are functionally recitational, although in other liturgical situa-

---

11. *The Early Middle Ages to 1300*, eds. Richard Crocker
and David Hiley, vol. 2 of *New Oxford History of Music*
(Oxford: Oxford University Press, 1990), 134.

tions (like the Gradual of the mass) the function is lyrical; both functions promote distinct musical styles. And attitudes towards psalmody have varied from an attentive subjectivity to an objective view of their recitation that makes little demand on the reciter's intention.

There is evidence that to the early church the psalm was, at least at times, received no differently than any scriptural lesson. In his *Confessions*, for example, Augustine recalls that

> We heard the Apostle [the Epistle], we heard the Psalm, we heard the Gospel; all the divine readings sound together so that we place hope not in ourselves but in the Lord.[13]

Here the psalm is a reading, in serial company with the Epistle and Gospel.

The literature of the desert fathers amply confirms the prominence of psalmody. In the *Life of St. Anthony* the desert communities were likened to tabernacles filled with saintly choirs reciting psalms, devoutly reading, fasting, praying, rejoicing in the hope of things to come, and laboring to give alms, while maintaining love and harmony among themselves. In the same source, all monks are enjoined to

> Flee vainglory and pray continuously; sing psalms before sleep and after sleep; store away the precepts of Scripture.[14]

---

12. I follow Elie Wiesel, *Souls on Fire* (New York: Vintage Books, 1972), 4-5. See also the epigram to his *The Gates of the Forest* (New York: Avon, 1966), a powerful evocation of the ritual "sufficiency" of "telling the story."

13. MECL, 161. See also Wainwright, *Doxology*, 211, for a confirming view.

14. MECL, 55

The psalms were sung while the monks labored as well as during what we would distinguish as "worship time." Such a fragmented view of time, however, is a more modern paradigm; to the monk seeking continuous prayer, often through the psalms, what time was not "worship"? The following tale is characteristic:

> The brothers told this story. We once visited some old men, and after the usual prayer we exchanged greetings and sat down. And after we had talked together, we made ready to go, and asked once again for prayer to be made. But one of the old men said to us: "What, have you not prayed already?" And we said: "Yes, father, when we came in, we prayed, and since then we have been talking." And he said "Forgive me, brothers; one brother, while he was sitting and talking with you, offered a hundred and three prayers" And with these words he prayed and sent us away.[15]

It is clear that the continuous prayer/recitation of the psalms locates a central activity for the early monks; it was contemplative and to be done with "understanding," as the following passage from the fourth-century Evagrius Ponticus makes clear:

> Pray with moderation and calm, and chant psalms with understanding and proper measure, and you will be raised on high like a young eagle.
> Psalmody lays the passions to rest and causes the stirrings of the body to be stilled.[16]

This is a significant passage in both its repeated emphasis on calm and stillness—the quiet of contemplation—and in its

15. In Owen Chadwick, *Western Asceticism*, 144.

16. *De Oratione* in MECL, 59.

openness to mystical heights ("raised on high like a young ea-
gle") as the outcome of such prayer "with understanding".

Psalmodic recitation and prayer has traditionally been
"with the lips," rendered physically as a joint venture between
body, mind, and spirit, interestingly conforming to medieval
norms of reading. Prior to the twelfth and early thirteenth centuries when the intellectual demands of scholasticism encouraged silent reading, reading was typically done aloud.[17]
Moreover, vocalized reading had antique roots. For example,
Cicero, slow to answer a letter, explains, "Please excuse me but
I have been unable to read your letter because my throat is
sore."[18] Though in early monastic communities the recitation
was from memory (and the physical vocalization was surely in
part an *aide memoire*), the link to the practice of reading
remains a compelling one. Dom Jean Leclercq has noted the
prayerfulness of reading aloud divine texts, "inscribing…the
sacred text in [*both*] the body and soul." He writes:

> The repeated mastication of the divine words [i.e. read-
> ing with the lips] is sometimes described by use of the
> theme of spiritual nutrition. In this case the vocabulary
> is borrowed from eating, from digestion, and from the
> particular form of digestion belonging to ruminants.
> For this reason, reading and meditation are sometimes
> described by the very expressive word *ruminatio*. For
> example, in praising a monk who prayed constantly Pe-
> ter the Venerable cried: 'Without resting, his mouth ru-
> minated the sacred words.' Of John of Gorze it was
> claimed that the murmur of his lips pronouncing the

17. For an extensive study, see Paul Saenger, "Silent Reading: Its Impact on Late Medieval Script and Society," *Viator: Medieval and Renaissance Studies* 13 (1982): 367-414.

18. Quoted in Ari L. Goldman, *The Search for God at Harvard* (New York: Ballantine Books, 1991), 252.

Psalms resembled the buzzing of a bee. To meditate is
to attach oneself closely to the sentence being recited
and weigh all its words in order to sound the depths of
their full meaning. It means assimilating the content of
a text by means of a kind of mastication which releases
its ful flavor. It means, as St. Augustine, St. Gregory,
John of Fecamp and others say in an untranslatable expression, to taste it with the *palatum cordis* or *in ore cordis*.[19]

What emerges in Leclercq's description is a type of reading that
is somatic as well as intellectual, the combination of which
leads the reader to a deep savoring of the text, perhaps especially memorable or present through its physicality. And we can
safely assume the somatic quality to be an important one.[20]
Even women constrained under Pauline prohibitions from offering the psalms aloud, nevertheless offered them somatically
with the lips active. In his *Procatechesis*, Cyril of Jerusalem states
that:

The assembly of virgins, however, should be gathered
together, quietly reciting psalms or reading, so that
their lips move, but the ears of others do not hear—
"For I do not permit that a woman speak in the
Church" (1 Cor. 14:34). And the married woman
should do likewise: she should pray and move her lips,
while not allowing her voice to be heard.[21]

19. See *The Love of Learning and the Desire for God*, 90.

20. In an interesting analogy, the fourteenth-century Eastern hesychast, St. Gregory Palamas promoted what one
recent writer has termed a "holistic anthropology," arguing
that "the body is called to share with the soul in the work of
prayer, just as it can share also in the vision of divine light."
See Henry Mayr-Harting, "The West: the Age of Conversion," in *The Oxford Illustrated History of Christianity*, 190.

Similarly, Caesarius of Arles urges that one pray in imitation of Hannah: "As she continued praying before the LORD, Eli observed her lips moved, and her voice was not heard…," i.e. silently, but with the lips engaged.[22]

We have seen something of the importance of the physical act of reciting to psalmody and we have seen caveats that urge the marriage of inner intention—"understanding"—with that physical act. That the caveats were issued in the first place may reasonably suggest that the ideal was not always attained, and, in some cases, it was perhaps not only unattained, but unintended as well. In the fifth-century *Consultationes Zachaei et Apollonii* various stages of monastic devotion are described with reference to psalmodic practice, the most fervent monks being those who would temporarily leave aside their continual prayer for the psalms; others in his description approach the psalms with no fervency. Jungmann comments:

> It thus appears that the rendering of the psalms was an external activity that did not count as one's real prayer. This seems true enough, as in the monastic arrangement for the Office it was a rule from the beginning to take the psalms simply in the order of the biblical Psalter, one after the other without regard to theme or connection, merely as sacral words proceeding from the mouth of God and returning to God, as though the sole purpose in view were the words themselves and a desire to find one's repose in them and thus to draw near God[23]

---

21. MECL, 75-76.

22. 1 Samuel 1: 12-13; Jungmann, *Christian Prayer*, 37.

23. Jungmann, *Christian Prayer*, 47.

It is easy to see the kindred relationship between this and a style
of flagging Renaissance churchmanship that encouraged non-
psalmodic schemes of meditation to accompany the recitation
of the psalms.[24]

The musical recitation of the psalms, in whatever form the
music takes, enhances the somaticism of the recitation, for
singing is a profoundly bodily act. We have tended to locate
music in intellectual or emotional strata that do little to
acknowledge the physicality of music as sound, especially significant in singing where the body is not only the channel for
reception, but the medium of production as well. John Shepherd, in his "Music, Text and Subjectivity" emphasizes that:

> Sound (and therefore music as text) is the only major
> channel of communication that actually vibrates inside
> the body. The sound of the voice could not be ampli-
> fied and projected were it not for chambers or resona-
> tors of air inside the human body (the lungs, the sinus
> passages, the mouth) that vibrate in sympathy with the
> frequencies of the vocal chords. Equally, the human ex-
> perience of sound involves, in addition to the sympa-
> thetic vibration of the eardrums, the sympathetic
> vibration of the resonators of the body. Sound is thus
> *felt* in addition to being 'heard.' Sound…is in the body
> and enters the body.[25]

Thus the singing of the psalms extends the concept of recita-

---

24. Cf. Jungmann: "We hear of abbot Garcia Cisneros (d.
1510) of Montserrat instructing his monks to meditate on
the successive events of the life and passion of Christ while
reciting the psalms of the choral office, which goes to show
that little or no spiritual nourishment was to be derived
from the psalms themselves." *Christian Prayer*, 127.

25. John Shepherd, *Music as a Social Text* (Cambridge: Polity Press, 1991), 179.

tion "with the lips," and in so doing, roots the psalm in the body as well as the mind and spirit.

Traditionally, and most enduringly, psalms have been chanted to short formulas known as "psalm tones." In the Gregorian repertory there are nine psalm tones, one for each mode and a "wandering" tone, the so-called *tonus peregrinus.*

Example 1. Psalm Tone Formulas

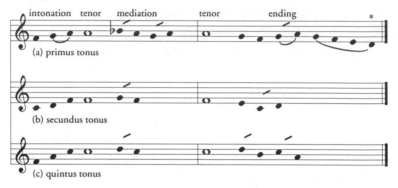

* A number of different endings are possible for most of the formulas

Example 1 shows several of these recitational formulas. All of the formulas feature, in the main, a reciting note of variable length (this the "tenor" from the Latin *tenere,* meaning to stretch out; this note corresponds to the dominant of the mode).   The reciting note is musically inflected with an introductory figure, the intonation, and two structural cadences. The resulting binary construction corresponds to the invariable division of psalm verses into two parts and, when sung at length, gives an undulating rise and fall remarkably akin to the rise and fall of meditative breathing.

The intonation, generally not repeated after the first verse, aurally identifies which psalm tone is to be sung. The tenor then provides the pitch for a monotonic recitation of the bulk of the text; cadence figures articulate each half verse. (Further inflection is possible. Intermediary *flexes,* downward falls from the monotone, occur where the text for the reciting note is

quite lengthy and requires subdivision—for sense and for respiration.) Thus the first two verses of psalm 4, *Cum invocarem,*
would be rendered as in Example 2 below.

Example 2. Psalm 4 *Cum invocarem* (vs. 1-2) Tone V

1. Cum in - vo - car - em, ex - au - di - vit me De - us jus - ti - ti - ae me - ae:

in tri - bu - la - ti - o - ne di - la - tas - ti mi - hi

2. Mi - se - re - re me - i et ex - au - di or - a - ti - o - nem me - am.

In no way does this suggest the psalm recitation as a lyrical moment. It is "musical" in only a minimal way, and it is "musical,"
i.e. "sung," I suspect for distinctly non-lyrical reasons, such as:

1.   to coordinate the reciting ensemble

2.   to ritualize the text

3.   to provide the somatic engagement that singing affords

4.   to aid the memory

Again, none of this suggests lyricism. However, the psalm *is* recited in conjunction with a lyric antiphon, a refrain sung in
some pattern of alternation with the verses, often framing
them. The texts for the antiphons are often from the psalms
themselves, underscoring a particular theme. In other instances, the antiphon texts are external to the psalms and offer
"proper" comment on the theme of the feast. For example, at
Vespers for Trinity Sunday, the antiphons hymn the praise of a
triune and eternal God:

> Glory to thee, O Trinity, co-equal, one-ly Deity, ere yet
> the worlds began to be, and now, and through eternity.

> Praise and unending glory resound from the lips of all
> men, to God the Father, and to the Son, and to the holy
> Paraclete, through ages everlasting.
> Etc.

The particularity of the antiphon does indeed enrich our sense
of liturgical time, i.e. it marks the circular trek through the calendar with familiar signposts, and it is didactic, underscoring
as it does, pertinent themes of the feast. But it is also, as an oc-
casional text, an illuminating counterpoint to the repeated, unchanging text of the psalm, whose verses, in context of a
particular antiphon, may lead one way, and in context of another antiphon, may lead elsewhere.

The antiphon chant, in contrast to the psalm tone, is lyrical—a melody—and the function of the antiphon, in part, is
to provide the vehicle for lyric response to recitation. The
dynamic resembles a "gathering" or a "collecting" in recitation
that seeks an outlet in the lyricism of the antiphon. It is a
familiar dynamic in prayer. The modern spiritual director
Robert Llewelyn of the St. Julian Shrine in Norwich describes
it with respect to the repeated recitation of the rosary in his
"Parable of the Pheasant."

> Once when living within the pleasant surrounding of
> a religious community I watched through my window
> a large and—it seemed to me—rather old pheasant on
> the lawn.
> It ran along the grass, took a short flight, and then,
> being tired, returned to earth once more. There fol-
> lowed a little more running, another flight and return,
> and so on.
> In that illustration we may see a parable of the saying
> of the rosary [or reciting of the psalms]. We move from
> one Hail Mary [psalm verse] to the next with such de-
> votion as God may give us, and then there may be, as it
> were, a short period on the wing [the antiphon]…and

somehow we are taken beyond [the words]…[i.e. into the lyricism, into the "music" of the antiphon.[26]

Dom Jean Leclercq expresses the same dynamic in an explicit context of art when he observes, "beauty has first to exist in our spirit and in our convictions [recitation] before it can be born in works of art [lyricism]."[27]

The "taking flight"—the transition from recitation to antiphon—is ideally as smooth as possible. To encourage this smoothness, most psalm tone formulas have various endings (*differentiae*, i.e. difference tones) to accommodate the ease of return to the antiphon. The second psalm for Trinity Vespers with its antiphon, "Laus et perennis gloria," is a good case in point.

Example 3. Tone II and Antiphon *Laus et perennis gloria*

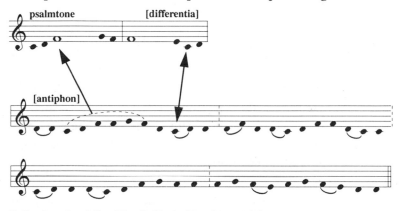

Following the *Liber Usualis* (Paris: Desclée, 1947)

As Example 3 shows, the *differentia* not only brings the singer

---

26. Robert Llewelyn, *A Doorway to Silence*   (New York: Paulist Press, 1986), 21.

27. See Leclercq, "*Otium Monasticum*," 75.

to the first note of the antiphon, but is also echoed in the cadence of the first phrase. A particularly strong link is forged between the first phrase of the antiphon and the intonation of the
psalm tone, echoed yet again in the third phrase of the antiphon. It is recurrent one suspects for both its common under-
pinning of the modal dominant as well as its link with the
psalm tone.

Thus far we have put forth a psalmodic practice that is

1. the heart of the Office
2. linked formatively with the continuous prayer
   of the early monks
3. both somatic as well as intellectual
4. given to the dynamic of lyrical expansion
   growing out of recitation.

It is at this juncture that we might profitably explore the
use of psalmodic recitation as a meditative or contemplative
technique—a process well served by the style of chant
described above. That the psalmodic recitation of the early
monks was contemplative is supported by remarks such as
those of Evagrius Ponticus quoted above (p. 47). The view persists in modern liturgical writing as well. The French Jesuit
composer Joseph Gelineau observes:

> Meditation, musically speaking, is that activity in
> which those who are celebrating consciously savour a
> text thanks to the use of rhythmic cadences and a more
> or less formalized tone pattern…. In Christian wor-
> ship, psalmody has been the most typical form of med-
> itation, and in its biblical sense, this always implies
> rumination upon words which are pronounced aloud.
> In this way, each person is 'informed,' possessed almost,
> by the inspired words he pronounces.[28]

Persistent repetition—such as the psalm tone formulas require—is conducive to meditation, as evidenced in the Christian tradition by the devotional use of the rosary and of so-called "breath prayer." The "saying" of the rosary combines cyclical repetition of a fixed prayer (the "Hail Mary") with mental reflection on the mysteries of Jesus' life, all tactilely impelled by fingering chained, prayer beads in succession. (The use of prayer beads is found in non-Christian traditions, as well.)

Similarly repetitive, "breath prayer" focuses on lengthy repetition of a short phrase, sometimes formed with the lips, and said in concert with the flow of respiration. Its most well known manifestation is the Eastern "Jesus Prayer", in which the petition "Lord Jesus Christ, have mercy on me" is continuously repeated as a means to inner stillness (*hesychasm*) and divine light. The Jesus Prayer is classically described in the nineteenth-century Russian work entitled *The Pilgrim*. Quoting from the *Philocalia*, it records:

> Take a seat in solitude and silence. Bend your head, close your eyes, and breathing softly, in your imagination, look into your own heart. Let your mind, or rather your thoughts, flow from your heart and say, while breathing: "Lord Jesus Christ, have mercy on me" Whisper these words gently, or say them in your mind. Discard all other thoughts. Be serene, preserving and repeat them over and over again.[29]

28. Joseph Gelineau, S.J., "Music and Singing in the Liturgy," in *The Study of the Liturgy*, 505.

29. In *A Treasury of Russian Spirituality*, ed. and comp. by George P. Fedotov (Belmont, Mass: Nordland, 1975), vol. 2, 288. Readers of J. D. Salinger will recognize the practice from its prominence in *Franny and Zooey* (New York: Little, Brown, 1961), passim.

Significantly the repetition here, or elsewhere, as in Hindustani mantric recitation or in the modern ostinato chants internationally popularized by the Monastery of Taizé, brings the one who prays into a context of circularity, with its attendant associations of sacred time and wholeness. The repeated prayer at its end, like the circle, finds itself back at its beginning. The linearity of rational, verbal syntax (and secular time) is replaced by the indwelling of the words in a continuous, circular act of savouring. The recitation of the psalms in the manner described above, though not literally repeating text, moves in this same contemplative mode, as its short "melodic" formulas continuously repeat, falling in cadence with the breath: this is music as a devotional *process.*

The amount of repetition that the process requires may be experienced as monotonous or tedious, especially by those accustomed to goal-oriented music. However, the monotony may be devotionally valuable. Fr. John-Julian Swanson, OJN, writing on the virtue of monotony in prayer observes:

> The true nobility of monotony is that it releases the internal energy of the mind which otherwise is being expended in appreciating, experimenting, understanding, and integrating the novelty of variety. Monotony tends to turn off the discursive and perceptive intellect and open the channels for something else.... The monotony of the mantric approach is a tool which ultimately flattens the rational and leaves space... for the intuitive."[30]

In other words, through the monotony of the repetition the singer gradually relinquishes mental control, creating room for the intuitive contemplation or experience of God.

Music as a meditative agent is familiar to us in a web of "inspirational," affective associations: the aesthetic musical

---

30. John-Julian Swanson, OJN, *Julian Jottings* (Waukesha, Wis.: Order of Julian of Norwich, [n.d.], no. 11, 4.

experience as theophany. But to consider music as a devotional process, we must broaden our way of thinking. Little of the psalm tone—itself not lyric—suggests affective response, nor does its largely uninflected mode of performance. Yet, this singing of the psalm, in its physical effects, may be particularly conducive to meditation somatically. This line of inquiry has received too little attention, though suggestions of its fruitfulness are near at hand. The widely read case studies of neurologist Oliver Sacks, for instance, powerfully underscore the physiological effects of music on the nervous system. In his moving account of patients with post-encephalitic Parkinsonism, he relates how recorded music would completely liberate one patient from her automatisms as the "jerking, ticcing, and jabbering" were replaced by a "blissful ease and flow of movement." Significantly, he observes that "this power of music to integrate and cure, to liberate the Parkinsonian and give him freedom while it lasts, is quite fundamental, and seen in every patient."[31] Similarly, the work of psychoacoustician Alfred A. Tomatis suggests that physiological effects are at work in meditative chanting.[32] (Recent writing on fasting suggests a compelling analogy with meditative music. Clearly both claim a strong somatic identity, though discussions have tended not to include the body. Theologian Margaret Miles writes, "Modern people, usually unfamiliar with the physical effects of fasting, often interpret the requirement of fasting in

---

31. See Oliver Sacks, *Awakenings* (New York: Harper Collins, 1973; 1990), 60. Sacks' clinical anthology *The Man Who Mistook His Wife for a Hat* (New York: Harper Collins, 1970; 1990) is also interesting in this regard.

32. See, for example, the audiotape by Tim Wilson, *Chant: the Healing Power of Voice and Ear* (Collegeville, Minn.:The Liturgical Press, [n.d.]) which reports on his interesting research.

ancient texts as representing rejection of the material world for
the spiritual world. Interpreting fasting in this way, however,
loses sight of the effect on the body and consciousness of short
fasts. We need to consider the possibility that Christian
authors were at least as interested in the effect of fasting as in
fasting as a symbolic statement.")[33]

The contemplative use of psalmodic recitation and the
liturgical psalm tones seem well matched indeed. However,
influences of time and place have at various times removed the
office from its contemplative associations. Like the Mass, the
Office, especially Vespers, could be a performance freighted
with aestheticism and the political circumstance of patron and
occasion. Concomitantly various musical styles, in addition to
the psalm tones, have found a home in office psalmody.
Changes in the musical style have been in the direction of
increasing the "musical" content. To the degree that we have
tied the contemplative process to sung *recitation*, these changes
in musical style accordingly may be seen to weaken that tie.

Among the first ways of rendering the recitation more
intrinsically "musical" was the harmonizing of the psalm tone
in the practice of *falsobordone* (faburden, fauxbourdon), arising
in the late fifteenth-century on the Continent. As a "musical"
development, its path was somewhat predictable, eventually
loosing its bonds from the cantus firmus (the chordal harmo-
nization of the psalm tone becomes a free chordal passage for
recitation), developing its expressive potential, and widening
its scope beyond liturgical psalmody.[34]

A particularly telling use of *falsobordone* is Gregorio Allegri's setting of the "Miserere mei" (Ps. 51), sung by the Cappella Sistina during Holy Week at Rome. In it we see several

33. See Margaret Miles, *Carnal Knowing: Female Nakedness
and Religious Meaning in the Christian West* (New York:
Vintage Books, 1989), 41-2.

increments of "musical" content, and with them a change in the nature of the psalm and its function. A rendition of a psalm with *falsobordone* would typically alternate monophonic chant (the psalm tone) with the *falsobordone*, verse by verse. Here Allegri gives us two different harmonizations—a four- and a five-voice version—which would alternate with the chant. To this richer mix of musical content is added overt expression. Giuseppe Santarelli (1710-90), quoted by Charles Burney, explicitly noted that certain words triggered changes in pace and that dynamic contrast was part of the work's performance, as was decorative embellishment. Santarelli, a member of the Cappella Sistina, observed, in Burney's words, that

> [the psalm's] beauty and effect arise more from the manner in which it is performed than from the composition—there are many stanzas to the same music—and the singers have by tradition certain customs and expressions and graces of convention, which produce great effects—such as swelling and diminishing the notes altogether; accelerating or retarding the measure, singing some stanzas quicker than others con certe expressioni e gruppi etc.[35]

These considerations significantly remove the psalm from a recitational context; it is *music and its attendant values* that have gained prominence here. Moreover, the aesthetic identity of the work was substantial and special enough that the Chapel could guard the setting as its exclusive property, and in so doing,

34. *Falsobordone* was used, for instance, by Schütz in the evangelist's role in the *Easter History* and as far afield as the secular madrigal by Monteverdi (see, e.g. "Sfogava con le stelle.")

35. Charles Burney, *Music, Men, and Manners in France and Italy 1770* (London: Eulenburg, 1974), 140.

spoke volumes about the objectification of a formerly subjective process.[36] In no way does this diminish the works *devotional* power, but it relocates it in the mode of aesthetic inspiration, not contemplative rumination, despite its origins in a recitational style.

There are other examples of making something "musical" of an essentially verbal recitation. Anglican chant, short bipartite chordal formulas for declamatory psalm singing, emerges in England as the *falsobordone* practice declines on the Continent,[37] and its development is a closely parallel one in many ways. Familiarly, Anglican chant begins as a harmonized version of a psalm tone in the tenor; with time the tie to a cantus firmus wanes and the upper voice, greater among equals, presents a free melody. This becomes the norm after the Restoration of the Monarchy in 1660, and still prevails at the height of Anglican chant activity in the nineteenth century.

---

36. Historians often relate the story of the young Mozart hearing the piece once and then copying it out from memory, thus challenging the Vatican monopoly. See, for example, Stanley Sadie, "Mozart, Wolfgang Amadeus," in *The New Grove Dictionary of Music and Musicians* (London: Macmillan, 1980), 12: 684.

37. For a standard discussion, see Peter le Huray, "Anglican Chant," in *The New Grove Dictionary of Music and Musicians,* 1: 430-31; Leonard Ellinwood, "From Plainsong to Anglican Chant" in *Cantors at the Crossroads* (St. Louis: Concordia, 1967); and Ruth Mack Wilson, "Anglican Chant and Chanting in England and America, 1660-1811," PhD diss, Illinois, 1988. The earliest source of Anglican chant is Thomas Morley's 1597 "how to" book, *A Plain and Easy Introduction to Music.* Early manuscript examples are recorded in the Peterhouse College Partbooks (c. 1635-1640). Though the chronology is suggestive of a linkage, evidence in support of Anglican chant as an imported *falsobordone* is lacking. See Wilson, "Anglican Chant," 56.

Example 4 below records several stages of the Anglican chant, ranging from the sixteenth-century tenor cantus firmus style to several "free" versions in different harmonic styles.

Example 4. Anglican Chants

(a) Thomas Morely, *A Plain & Easy Introduction* (1597)

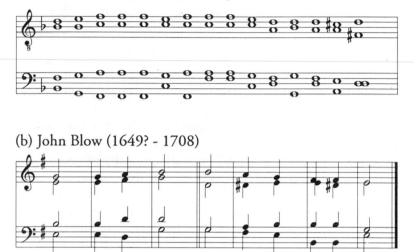

(b) John Blow (1649? - 1708)

(c) W.H. Longhurst (1819 - 1904)

When speaking of the dynamic between recitation and lyric antiphon, I proposed that the recitation was a time of "collection" from which one "took flight" into the lyricism of the antiphon. The progress is, in this context, successive:

recitation $\rightarrow$ flight $\rightarrow$ recitation $\rightarrow$ flight

ps. tone $\rightarrow$ antiphon $\rightarrow$ ps. tone $\rightarrow$ antiphon

The act is a composite one requiring both modes to bring it to a sense of completion. What the harmonized recitations seem to have done, be they Anglican chant or *falsobordone*, is to have taken the *successive* components and rendered them *simultaneously*, as the harmony's relationship to the recitation corresponds to that of the plainsong antiphon and its associated recitation. In both, the recitation is dynamically joined to lyricism; the presence of the lyrical element may be intermittent, as in a repeating antiphon, or constant, as in the invariable presence of harmony. This functional equivalence of harmony and antiphon is hinted at in the writing of Dom Anselm Hughes, a prominent medievalist and one-time prior of Nashdom Abbey:

> After 30 years of working plainsong, I have come slowly but surely to believe that *good* Anglican chanting is a perfect musical expression of the English Psalter. *Plainsong psalms, for a similar degree of perfection must have their antiphons or they are like a body which has no skin.*[38]

The Office, especially Vespers, has in various circumstances been a "concert" liturgy, with the central act of "doing" replaced by watching and listening to someone else "do". And in this context, the liturgical musical style has been fully

---

38. "Anglican chant" in Oxford *Companion to Music* (London: Oxford University Press, 1972), 35. Emphasis added.

sophisticated and professional. The context admits a wide range of interpretations. At one extreme, the liturgy, with its professional music, is spectator sport, casting musical essays in established forms, hallowed with age and circumstance, but not necessarily hallowed by intent. At the other extreme is devout, though passive, participation in the liturgical actions of surrogates. Here, to return to a central point, the music may powerfully incite devotion affectively and aesthetically, but has done so through "inspiration," not devotional process.

"Concert" settings of Vespers are common in a variety of periods from the Renaissance through the late eighteenth century, and include works by the leading composers of the day. Familiar examples include Mozart's Vesperae de Dominica, K 321 and Vesperae solennes de Confessore, K 339, Vesper psalms by Handel (likely comprising a "Carmelite Vesper"),[39] and Monteverdi's Vespers of 1610. Such works are often motivated by commemorative occasions, votive intent, and/or patronal display. For instance, it is difficult to veil the splendor of the Gonzagas that shines through the pages of Monteverdi's work, never more so than in the opening versicle and response where the fanfare from *Orfeo*—a family salute?—is transformed into an ecclesiastical curtain raiser. In this case, historians are inconclusive regarding the occasion which prompted such display. One recent theory has placed it speculatively at the pontifical vespers sung at the inauguration of a new order of knighthood in Mantua, connected with the wedding celebration of Francesco Gonzaga and Margherita of Savoy. Both

---

39. See J. S. Hall, "Handel among the Carmelites," *Dublin Review* 233 (1959): 121-131, and "The Problem of Handel's Latin Church Music, *Musical Times* 100 (1959): 197-200; and, more recently, Graham Dixon, "Handel's music for the Carmelites," *Early Music* 15 (1987): 16-29.

the commemorative nature and patronal importance would suggest a work on this scale and of this "concert" nature.[40]

The psalm settings of Monteverdi's Vespers are elaborate ensemble pieces, full of "modern" concertato effects, which colorfully bring in to play virtuosic solo lines and rich choral textures (up to eight voices) with obligatto and colla parte instruments. Significantly, although the psalms are modern, sophisticated, and musically eventful—sometimes dazzlingly so—they are also grounded in psalm tone cantus firmus. *Dixit Dominus*, for instance, uses Psalm tone IVa as both an imitative subject and as a structural bass line supporting a fashionable treble duet. The presence of the psalm tones in Monteverdi's settings secure for them a readily identifiable link with the tradition of Office recitation. They are rarely recitative, with the exception of a few passages of *falsobordone* in *Dixit Dominus*; their effect and intent is *musical*. But the choice of cantus firmus associatively brings to mind the style and function of recitation.

Monteverdi has not set antiphons for these psalm settings, and one would generally assume a chant antiphon would frame the concerted psalm. However, Monteverdi's 1610 publication interleaves solo vocal concertos between the psalms, suggesting that they are antiphon substitutes.[41] Importantly, as antiphon substitutes, they provide a similar "flight" into lyr-

---

40. Iain Fenlon, "The Monteverdi Vespers: Suggested Answers to Some Fundamental Questions," *Early Music* 5 (1977): 380-87. Graham Dixon has suggested the Vespers might have been performed in celebration of the Feast of St. Barbara in the Gonzaga ducal chapel, a chapel under her patronage; see "Monteverdi's Vespers of 1610: della Beata Virgine?" *Early Music* 15 (1987): 386-89.

41. See Stephen Bonta, "Liturgical Problems in Monteverdi's Marian Vespers," *Journal of the American Musicological Society,* 20 (1967): 87-106.

icism that we have earlier associated with plainsong antiphons. The psalms here are admittedly not recitative, but they are corporate, ensemble expressions, somewhat abstract in nature because of their use of cantus firmus. The concertos, on the other hand, are intensely personal texts, some with amatory imagery from the Song of Solomon.

In full accord with the intimacy of the concerto texts, the musical style is full of affective mannerism and individualized expression. For example, the concerto *Duo Seraphim* presents Isaiah's mystical vision of the cosmic temple, full of the voices of angels. In the opening of the concerto, it is difficult to miss the ecstasy of angelic rapture in the highly sensual chain of suspensions. And canonic melismata teem with excitement as they underscore "the earth is full of your glory." As highly subjectivized moments they are powerful instances of intimate, lyrical release or "flight," growing out of the activity of the more abstract, corporate psalm. It is a dynamic central to the psalmodic core of the Office, and here we see it again transcending the particularity of style.

4

THE MASS

When the hour came, he took his place at the table, and the apostles with him. He said to them, "I have eagerly desired to eat this Passover with you before I suffer; for I tell you, I will not eat it until it is fulfilled in the kingdom of God." Then he took a cup, and after giving thanks he said, "Take this and divide it among yourselves; for I tell you that from now on I will not drink of the fruit of the vine until the kingdom of God comes." Then he took a loaf of bread, and when he had given thanks, he broke it and gave it to them saying, "This is my body, which is given for you. Do this in remembrance [anamnesis] of me." And he did the same with the cup after supper, saying, "This cup that is poured out for you is the new covenant in my blood." (Luke 22: 14-20).[1]

PRIOR to his crucifixion, Jesus of Nazareth took the passover meal with his disciples gathered in an upper room in Jerusalem. Within the ritual context of this passover meal, Jesus estab-

1. Cf. Matthew 26: 26-28, Mark 14: 22-25, and 1Cor. 11: 23-26.

lished a mystical identity between himself and the bread and the wine—they become his body and blood—and ensured the continuity of the communion with his command, "Do this in remembrance of me." [2] "Doing this in remembrance" is the central act of the Christian liturgical community. Known variously as the "Mass," the "Eucharist," "Holy Communion," or the "Lord's Supper," it consists of four basic ritual components:

1. the gathering of the community
2. the hearing of its story
3. the offering and blessing of bread and wine
4. the consuming of them as Christ.

Although these components are fundamental, the ceremonial through which they are rendered and the interpretation of the liturgical action involved is historically varied.

In considering the nature of the mass, one key concept is the approach to time indicated by the Greek word *anamnesis*. In the passage from Luke's Gospel, above, "remembrance" is originally *anamnesis*, connoting a more complex idea than simply memory or recollection. *Anamnesis* is the making present of something which is past. To "remember" is to recall a past event that is absent; in *anamnesis* however, this quality of absence does not occur. Thus, Dom Gregory writes:

> It [*anamnesis*] is not quite easy to represent accurately in English, words like 'remembrance' or 'memorial' having for us a connotation of something itself *absent*, which is only mentally recollected. But in the scriptures

---

2. Regarding the authenticity of the phrase "Do this in remembrance of me," see SL, 64-70. For more recent discussion, see Joachim Jeremias, *The Eucharistic Words of Jesus*, trans. Norman Perrin (London: SCM, 1966), and Nils A. Dahl, "Anamnesis: Memory and Commemoration in Early Christianity," in *Jesus in the Memory of the Early Church* (Minneapolis: Augsburg, 1976), 11-29.

both of the Old and New Testament, *anamnesis* and the cognate verb have the sense of 're-calling' or 're-presenting' before God an event in the past, so that it becomes *here and now operative by its effects*.[3]

In this way, the *anamnesis* of Jesus' sacrificial passion, an event in past historical time, is made eternally present in the ritual of the mass. In a similar vein, Carl Jung addresses the "inner meaning" of the consecration as "the revelation of something existing in eternity, a rending of the veil of temporal and spatial limitations which separates the human spirit from the sight of the eternal."[4]

The mass then makes Jesus' sacrifice "present": the breaking of the bread is the breaking of his body for the atonement of sins. And in Catholic thought, the eucharistic offering of the church *continues* the sacrifice of Jesus, though neither challenging its uniqueness or sufficiency. However, Reformation traditions, some of which interpret the eucharist as a "memorial," strongly repudiate this Roman notion of sacrifice. Luther, for example, writes in *The Babylonian Captivity of the Church* (1520): "The third captivity of this sacrament is by far the most wicked abuse of all, in consequence of which there is no opinion more generally held or more firmly believed in the church today than this, that the mass is a good work and a sacrifice."[5]

In order to see in the Mass the *anamnesis* and oblation of Jesus' sacrifice, the bread and the wine (in themselves also offerings to God) must become mystically his body and blood.

---

3. SL, 161.

4. Jung, "Transformation Symbols," 103.

5. In *Luther's Works*, gen. ed. Helmut T. Lehmann (Philadelphia; Muhlenberg Press, 1959), 36: 35.

This "transubstantiation" was a point of contention between the Reformers and the Church of Rome. And the nature of Christ's presence in the sacrament—"real" or "symbolic"—was closely intertwined with views of the Eucharist as sacrifice or memorial. So, in varying degrees, the eucharist is an *anamnesis* of the sacrifice of Jesus' passion in the form of a holy meal, the elements of which are Christ, symbolically or substantially. And the sharing of the holy meal is one form in which Christ's presence is perpetuated among the community of believers; they are brought into "communion" with Him and with one another.

The nature of the liturgy has varied with time, an interesting foil to the stability of much of its text. Jungmann confirms that the oldest texted documents are from the eighth and ninth centuries, and cites the difficulty of reading them "backwards" any earlier than the sixth. But, he underscores that "for the most part whatever is here transmitted as the permanent text—especially the canon [prayer of consecration], but likewise the major portion of the variable prayers of the celebrant, and the readings—is almost identical with present-day [sic 1951] usage."[6] Again, this element of stability—an enduring textual core—stands in strong contrast to the changing nature of the eucharistic liturgy. The eucharist in the early church was a gathering of the community of believers in which the at one-time improvised prayers and exhortations of their ordained presider combined with the active voice of the believers themselves, a concerted action in which everyone played a distinctive part. Later, medieval developments, especially under Frankish leadership transform the eucharistic liturgy into essentially a priestly exercise, in private or in community. This

6. Joseph Jungmann, SJ, *The Mass of the Roman Rite: Its Origins and Development*, [MRR] vol. 1 (1949; Eng. trans.New York: Benziger Bros., 1951), 49.

"dissolution of the liturgical community" (Klauser) saw the priest celebrate within a visual privacy with his back to the community. And he spoke in whispers from within aural sanctuary of hushed silence. Both diminish the activity of the community. So much so that, with the ascendancy of the private mass, a development born of the swell of monastic ordinations to the priesthood, it became altogether expendable. In the private mass, the priest and his single server offer the sacrifice alone as an act of private devotion. Communion, in the sense of a shared, holy meal, has become here a communion of contemplative adoration.

The advent of the private mass says much about the evolving nature of the eucharistic liturgy. It does not say all, however, for it coexisted with the solemn high mass, a dramatic corporate display full of intricate medieval panoply, aesthetically and spiritually one of the great achievements of the Middle Ages. It is indeed a corporate action—an ensemble performance of a community—but the ensemble is distinctively a clerical one. The "action" of the community of believers is visual adoration. The visual paradigm is most clearly enshrined in the practice of elevation, an innovative ritual action arising in thirteenth-century Paris in which at the consecration the sacred elements are held aloft by the priest, momentarily abandoning his visual privacy, as a bell summons the onlookers worshipfully to attend the Real Presence now in their midst: a climactic moment of mystical awe. As Jungmann aptly notes: "The *eucharista* has become an *epiphania*, an advent of God who appears amongst men and dispenses His graces."[7] The spiritual food of the holy meal has become the Divine King enthroned upon the altar. That which was near and taken within is seen and worshipped from afar.

---

7. MRR, 117.

The form of the mass admits regional variability of detail and certainly shows chronological development.[8] However, a certain form preserved in eleventh-century sources emerges as traditional and long-lived, essentially in place until the reforms of Vatican II. The table below details its form with reference to the functional components outlined on p. 69. (P=Proper; O=Ordinary)

THE SYNAXIS (or "foremass", or "mass of the catechumens")
The community gathers

Introit (P)	an antiphonal psalm, once the procession of the ministers
Kyrie (O)	a nine-fold plea for mercy (in Greek), a remnant of an earlier litany
Gloria (O)	an expansion of the angelic hymn of praise found in the Lukan account of the Nativity. Omitted in penitential seasons
Oratio (collect) (P)	a short prayer by the celebrant "collecting" the prayers of the people (from a now missing litany?) into a summary

The community hears its story: readings and responses

Epistle (P)	a reading from the New Testament letters
Gradual (P)	a responsorial psalm in response to the reading

---

8. Chronological developments of the mass are summarized in tabular form in Harper, *Forms and Orders* 112, and, with geographic distinctions, in SL 442a, 475.

Epistle (P)	a reading from the New Testament letters
Alleluia (P)	a responsorial psalm in response to the reading (Penitential seasons substitute the Tract)
Sequence	a regional accretion in verse appended to the alleluia
Gospel (P)	a reading from one of the four gospels of the New Testament
Homily	a sermon expounding on the readings, especially the Gospel
Credo (O)	the "Nicene Creed," a dogmatic summary of the faith, voiced here as the community's assent to that which has preceded

THE EUCHARIST (or "sacrifice mass" or "mass of the faithful")
The community offers gifts of bread and wine

Offertory (P)	an antiphon, the remnant of a full antiphonal psalm that had accompanied an offertory procession in which bread and wine and other gifts were presented
Secret (P)	silent prayers of the priest in preparation for offering the sacrifice

The Community, through the action of the priest, blesses the bread and wine

Preface (P)	a dialogue to unite all, both the angelic and earthly choir in the act of praise which follows
Sanctus (O)	the ceaseless hymn of the angels, based on Isaiah's mystical vision of the cosmic temple (Isaiah 6: 3). It here not only offers praise, but establishes that the liturgy takes place at both the heavenly and the earthly altar
Canon (O)	priest's prayer of consecration of the bread and wine, centering on Jesus' words of institution
Pater Noster (O)	the Lord's Prayer, emphasizing both daily bread and forgiveness in anticipation of the communion to follow

The bread is broken and shared

The fraction/Agnus (O)	the bread is broken while the Agnus Dei is sung, a song in which Christ is addressed as the "Lamb of God," underscoring the sacrificial nature of the fraction and the Passover context of Christ's sacrifice
The Communion (P)	an antiphon, the remnant of a full antiphonal psalm, is sung as the host is consumed
Post Communion (P)	a recited prayer

The Community is dismissed

Ite, missa   a versicle and response of dismissal
est (O)

The two-part form of the mass (synaxis and eucharist) reflects different liturgical functions as well as different communities within the church. The first part, the "synaxis" (=public meeting) resembles patterns of Jewish prayer and, collaterally, the Divine Office. Its didactic emphasis on scripture addresses not only the "initiated" faithful of the assembly, the baptized, but also the *catechumens*, neophytes learning the faith in preparation for baptism, traditionally at the Great Vigil of Easter.[9]   The second half, the eucharist proper, is the sacramental action of the initiated faithful alone, distinct in both its character—sacramental and mystical—and in its constituency—the baptized. (Prior to the sixth century the catechumens were formally dismissed at the end of the synaxis.) In both halves the liturgy unfolds a drama: the church's scriptural history in the synaxis and the sacrifice of Jesus in the eucharist. Each drama dynamically moves to a climax: Jesus' presence in the reading of the Gospel and his presence in the eucharistic sacrifice. The response both to and within the drama inflects and colors its unfolding in a close-knit weave of gesture, sight, and sound... and great beauty, a beauty beyond the claims of aesthetic worth that the individual parts may assert.

---

9. For an important account of the catechumenate, see Egeria's record of her pilgrimage in Jerusalem. *Egeria: Diary of a Pilgrimage*, esp. 122–125.

THE SYNAXIS
The Gathering: Introit, Kyrie, Gloria, Collect

I was glad when they said to me, "Let us go to the house of the Lord." (Ps. 122: 10)

Introit—When Moses faced the burning bush of the Lord on Mt. Horeb, the Lord said to him:

> Come no closer! Remove the sandals from your feet, for the place on which you are standing is holy ground. (Exodus 3: 5)

The church, the sanctuary of God, continues this holy ground of Mt. Horeb. And because of this, the entry into the holy ground of the church was not only a physical, practical action accompanied by music—the introit—but also a richly symbolic spiritual movement. This formal entrance into the church is indeed a procession, a parade, from one location to another— from the vestry to the altar—but it is also a spiritual movement from the secular to the sacred.[10] And this procession is, as Robert Markus notes, like the "journey of salvation":

> The church building was a microcosm of the heavenly kingdom. To enter a church was to enter a world separated from the work-a-day environment by its interior layout, its decor, all designed to enhance the sense of

---

10. Cf. Eliade, *Sacred and Profane*, 25. On processions in general, cf. van der Leeuw, *Sacred and Profane Beauty*, 39– 40: "Especially in processions we find a latent awareness of the rhythmic background of life; when things are serious, we do not simply run to and fro in confusion, but group ourselves according to a definite, conventional order...Whenever we feel the need for the consolidation of life, we subject ourselves once again to rhythm."

the saint's solemn presence in his shrine. To walk the
length of a great basilica from porch to apse was to
make the journey of salvation and find oneself in 'a
place of perfection, the heavenly Jerusalem, its walls
and buildings made in heaven, transferred to this
spot.'[11]

Thus, one moves into a space that is objectively holy, a "micro-
cosm of the heavenly kingdom." Yet Jesus was clear that the
kingdom of God was an *inner* kingdom, a kingdom *within*
(Luke 17: 21). Modern comment on the subjective reaction to
space illumines the connection between the building—as
shape—and the soul's "heavenly kingdom." Keith Critchlow, a
London architectural designer, significantly observes:

> Whenever a person enters an interior space, part of
> himself or herself becomes the shape of that space; it is
> a very remarkable thing and most people experience
> this, whatever their interest. The shape of the room be-
> comes extremely important in a particular and subtle
> sense. So, from that point of view, the building is not
> removed from you; you can have an experience of how
> you actually *are* the building, and that is what a sacred
> building can do for a person.[12]

One enters the holy and, in a subjective sense, becomes holy.
The introit then is a liturgical *process* of transition, affording a
motion from place to place. Accordingly then, certain introits
which employ texts of motion or give a heightened sense of

11. Robert Markus, "From Rome to the Barbarian
Kingdoms (330–700)," in *Oxford Illustrated History of
Christianity*, 80.

12. "The Golden Proportion: A Conversation between
Richard Temple and Keith Critchlow." *Parabola* 16, no. 4
(1991): 32.

place are especially resonant with function, as the examples below suggest:[13]

Introit texts of motion

Feast	Text
Saturday after Lent IV	[*Sitientes, venite*] All you that thirst, come to the waters, saith the Lord: and you that have no money, come and drink with joy…(Isaiah 55: 1)
Wednesday in Easter Week	[*Venite, benedicti*] Come, ye blessed of My Father, possess you the kingdom, alleluia, prepared for you from the foundation of the world, alleluia, alleluia, alleluia…Matthew 25: 34)

Introit texts of place

Thursday after Lent I	[*Confessio et pulchritudo*] Praise and beauty are before Him: holiness and majesty in His sanctuary…(Ps. 96: 6)
Pentecost VIII	[*Suscepimus, Deus*] We have received Thy mercy, O God, in the midst of Thy temple…(Ps. 48: 8)
Pentecost XI	[*Deus in loco sancto*] God in His holy place: God who maketh men of one mind to dwell in a house… (Ps. 68: 36))

---

13. Translations follow *St. John's Missal*….(New York: Brepols' Catholic Press, [1952]).

In addition to offering in some cases highly resonant texts evoking motion and place, some offer strong summaries of the
theme of the day. In these cases, the introit impells motion not
only into sacred space, but into the theme of the day as well.

Thematic Introits

Ascension   [*Viri Galilaei*] Ye men of Galilee, why mar-
                 vel ye, looking up into heaven? alleluia: He
                 shall so come as ye have seen Him going up
                 into heaven: alleluia, alleluia, alleluia. (Acts
                 1: 11)

Pentecost   [*Spiritus Domini*] The Spirit of the Lord
                 hath filled the whole earth, alleluia; and that
                 which containeth all things hath knowledge
                 of the voice, alleluia, alleluia, alleluia. (Wis-
                 dom 1: 7)

Trinity   [*Benedicta sit sancta*] Blessed be the Holy
                 Trinity and undivided Unity; we will give
                 glory unto Him, because He hath shown us
                 His mercy. (Tobias 12: 6)

The music for the introit is an antiphonal psalm, conforming to the description of this kind of psalmody in Chapter
Three, viz. a lyric refrain alternating with a psalm tone verse.
The early papal model for the introit suggests a lengthy procession. A description from an eighth-century Roman Ordo
gives a good sense of the color and extent of the moment:

> [T]he subdeacon-attendant stands before the pontiff
> until such time as the latter shall sign to him that they
> may sing the psalm. As soon as the signal is given, he
> immediately goes out before the doors of the sacristy,
> and says, *Light up!* And as soon as they have lit their

candles the subdeacon-attendant takes the golden censer and puts incense in it in front of the sacristy doors,
so that he may walk before the pontiff. And the ruler of
the choir passes through the presbytery to the precentor
or the succentor or vice-succentor, and bowing his head
to him says, *Sir, command!*

Then they rise up and pass in order before the altar, and
the two rows arrange themselves in this manner: the
men-singers on either side without the doors [of the
presbytery], and the children on each side within. Immediately the precentor begins the anthem [antiphon
to the introit] for the entry: and when the deacons hear
his voice, they at once go to the pontiff in the sacristy.
Then the pontiff, rising, gives his right hand to the
archdeacon, and his left to the second [deacon] or who-
ever may be appointed: who, after kissing his hands,
walk with him as his supporters. Then the subdeacon-
attendant goes before him with the censer, diffusing the
perfume of incense: and the seven collets of the district
which is responsible for that day, carrying seven lighted
candlesticks, go before the pontiff to the altar. But before they arrive at the altar, the deacons put off their
plancts in the presbytery, and the district-deacon takes
them and gives each severally to a collet of the district
to which each deacon belongs. Then two collets approach, holding open pixes containing the Holy Element; and the subdeacon-attendant, taking them, with
his hand in the mouth of the pix, show the Holy Element to the pontiff and the deacon who goes before
him. Then the pontiff and the deacon salute the Holy
Element with bowed head, and look at the same in order that if there be too many fragments he may cause
some of them to be put in the aumbry. After this the
pontiff passes on, but before he comes to the choir the
bearers of the candlesticks divide, four going to the
right and three to the left; and the pontiff passes be-

tween them to the upper part of the choir, and bows his
head to the altar. He then rises up, and prays, and
makes the sign of the cross on his forehead; after which
he gives the kiss of peace to one of the hebdomadary
bishops, and to the archpresbyter, and to all the deacons. Then turning towards the precentor, he signs to
him to sing, *Glory be to the Father, and to the Son, etc.*
[the end of the psalm]; and the precentor bows to the
pontiff, and begins it. Meantime the ruler of the choir
precedes the pontiff in order to set his faldstool before
the altar, if it should be the season for it: and approaching it, the pontiff prays thereat until the repetition of
the verse [i.e. the anthem [antiphon] for the entry].
Now when *As it was in the beginning* is said, the deacons
rise up in order to salute the sides of the altar, first two,
and then the rest by twos, and return to the pontiff.
And then the latter arises, and kisses the book of the
gospels and the altar, and, going to his throne, stands
there facing eastwards. [14]

Obviously this was a ceremonial action of great richness,
and the flexible length psalmody—the Pope gives a signal
when he is through—was an important component.

For various reasons, however, this lengthy ceremonial
action "lost its action." As a result, the chant by the eleventh-
century, and in someplaces as early as the eighth, was reduced
to the antiphon with a single verse and the Gloria Patri. The
development of musical form may have contributed to the
abbreviation of the text—"developed" forms take longer to
sing and thus less text is needed—but also the arrangement of
new church buildings was influential. Some diminished the

---

14. *Ordo Romanus Primus* in *The Library of Liturgiology &
Ecclesiology for English Readers*, vol. 6 (London: The De la
More Press, 1905), 126-131.

distance to the altar; others had inadequate space for elaborate processions.[15] Thus the solemn procession into the Holy of Holies is reduced to a short trek to the altar at the end of an abbreviated chant, or, indeed, the truncated introit accompanies no procession at all, but rather "covers" the preparatory prayers of the priest *at* the altar.

This truncation and elimination of action we will also see in the other antiphonal chants of the Mass, the Offertory and the Communion. Changes such as these show the liturgy to be a living form. This particular change obviously affected the musical content in a very tangible way: a radical reduction of its length. But it also changed the nature of its contribution to the introit *process*. As developed above, the chief function of the introit appears to be a spiritual transition; a transition that was dramatically embodied in the *physical* act of procession. The introit chant was accompanimental to this action. Once the entry of the ministers ceased to be a procession, however, what happened to the *physical embodiment* of this spiritual transition? Arguably, the succession of tones in the introit chant—a *motion* in linear time—now fills this function to a degree. In other words, the music now must embody the motion of stilled feet to give a physical corollary to the spiritual motion. In this sense, then, the music of the truncated introit has become even more critical to the liturgical function, even though its most obvious justification—music to walk to—has become nullified. Accompanimental walking music is now a critical mode of transition.

---

15. I follow MRR 1: 323-324. Regarding the development of musical form, it is significant that the Introit was a favorite location in the Mass for the embellished additions of troping.

Kyrie—Two choral chants of the Ordinary follow: the Kyrie and the Gloria. The Kyrie is a tripartite formula invoking the mercy of Christ.

Kyrie eleison (Lord, have mercy)	3 times
Christe eleison (Christ, have mercy)	3 times
Kyrie eleison	3 times

This formula is rooted in *litanies*, a form of prayer in which a varying petition (or petitionee) is followed by a fixed response. Thus, from the ancient litany of saints:

....

Sancta Maria,	*ora pro nobis* (pray for us)
Sancta Virgo virginum,	*ora pro nobis*
Sancte Michael,	*ora pro nobis*
Sancte Gabriel,	*ora pro nobis*
Sancte Raphael,	*ora pro nobis*

A common and long standing response was "Kyrie eleison" described in fourth-century sources from both Jerusalem and Antioch.[16] And though litanies themselves did not endure in the mass ceremonial, their echo lingers in the entrance ceremonies.

The tripartite repetitions are resonant with the intrinsic wholeness/holiness of the number three. At various times tertian symbolism has been rationalized with reference to the

---

16. MRR 1: 334.

Holy Trinity and to the fact that three is the smallest integer to have a beginning, a middle, and an end (wholeness).

Gloria—The Kyrie is immediately followed by the Gloria, a joyful text whose affection is a striking balance to the supplicative Kyrie, though at the same time a text whose strong Trinitarian construction extends the tertian resonance of the previous chant, as it does in part also the pleas for mercy to Jesus. The Trinitarian construction is outlined below:

GLORIA

God the Father

Glory be to God in the highest. And on earth peace to men of good will. We praise Thee. We bless Thee. We adore Thee. We glorify Thee. We give thanks for thy great glory. O Lord God, heavenly King, God the Father, Almighty.

Lord, God, Son of the Father

O Lord, Jesus Christ, the only-begotten Son, O Lord, God, Lamb of God, Son of the Father. Who takest away the sins of the world, have mercy on us. Who takest away the sins of the world, receive our prayer, Who sittest at the right hand of the Father, have mercy on us. For thou alone art holy, Thou alone art the Lord. Thou alone, O Jesus Christ, art most high,

Holy Spirit

together with the Holy Spirit, in the glory of God the Father. Amen.

The Gloria's acceptance into the liturgy was incremental, initially reserved to the bishop's mass and that only at high feasts, though by the eleventh century, it was common in all masses in non-penitential seasons. This seasonal omission during Advent and Lent as well as at Requiems demonstrates again the way music colors the context. That it was proper to omit it at these times suggests its affective particularity, enhanced by associations with Christmas—the opening phrases "repeat the sounding joy" of the angels at Bethlehem. And one scholar has interestingly suggested that its "lively swing" played a role in making its acceptance only gradual:

> One gets the impression that the lively swing of this certainly very popular hymn did not seem quite suitable to the celebrants who were responsible for the services, for it did not conform in any way to their ideas of what constituted a dignified liturgy.[17]

The joy of the Gloria is, for centuries, more a function of its text rather than its music. Although modern ears will quickly recall the unbridled *glory* of Glorias by Monteverdi, Vivaldi, and Bach, with their vigorous dotted rhythms, buoyant octave leaps, and swirling trumpet arpeggios, it is important to remember that pre-Baroque music in general, and chant in particular, is affectively much less explicit. In this regard then, it is interesting to note that some Renaissance Glorias are most explicitly affective not in the texts of joy, but of supplication. The low, dark chordal sonorities of Ockeghem's *Missa Mi Mi* at "suscipe deprecationem nostram" (receive our prayer) are a good case in point, as the music seems to "fall on its knees." (Example 5 on page 88-89)

More vivid perhaps is Josquin's treatment of "miserere nobis" (have mercy upon us) and "suscipe..." in his famous *Missa Pange Lingua*. Both phrases receive slow, chordal declamations in response to contrapuntal statements of "Qui tollis peccata mundi." (who takest away the sins of the world). Their

17. Klauser, *Short History,* 83.

textural similarity allows them to be heard as litany-like refrains. In both Glorias, Ockeghem and Josquin have chosen to make the supplicative especially memorable and affective.

Collect—The collect appears to be the concluding prayer of the now missing litany whose "Kyrie" refrain lingers in the beginning of the mass.[18] Litanies would require a summary prayer by the celebrant, "collecting" the preceding petitions into a unified statement. And it is this summary prayer which the collect offers. The last of the events in the "gathering of the community," its act of collection—of bringing together—is significant as a gesture of *inclusion*, as if to confirm that much as the petitions are now focussed in one prayer, so too is the community physically and spiritually "collected" in one ecclesial body.

The form of the collect is characteristically a direct address followed by an amplifying relative clause—often here the theme of the day is underscored—and then the petition, as the examples below show:

---

18. MRR 1: 265.

Example 5. Johannes Ockeghem *Missa Mi Mi*, "Gloria" (mm. 64–96).

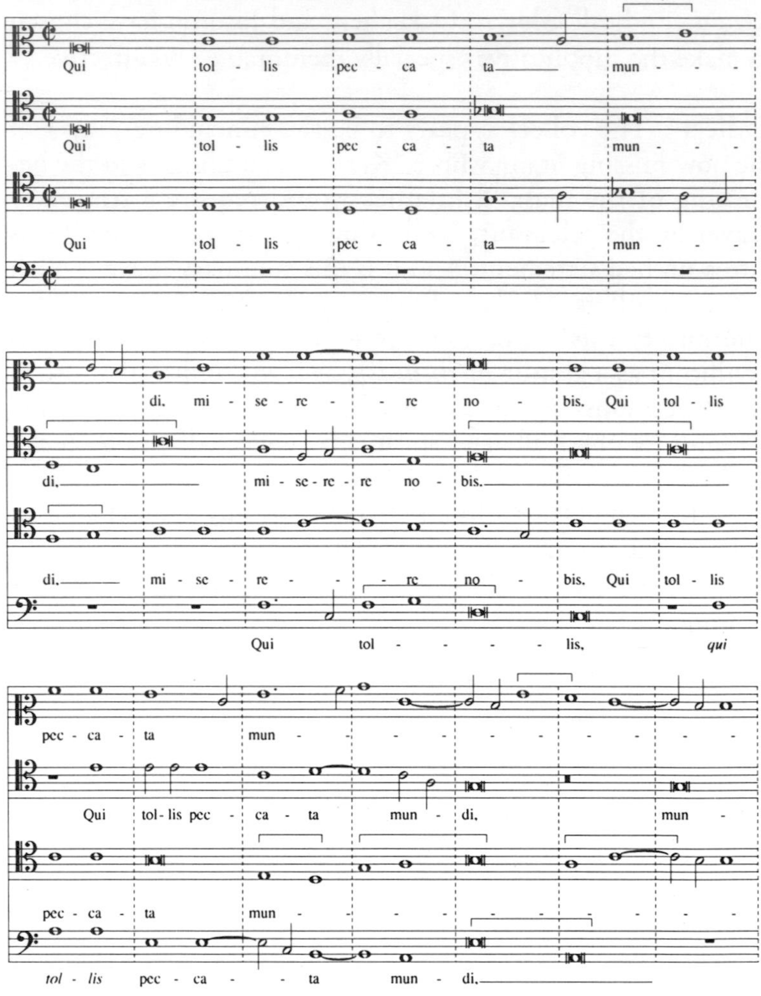

Johannes Ockeghem, *Collected Works*, ed. by Dragan Plamenac (New York: Galaxy Music, 1959), 2:4–5. Used by permission.

Vigil of the Nativity

> O God [DIRECT ADDRESS], who gladdenest us
> with this yearly expectation of our redemption [THE-
> MATIC RELATIVE CLAUSE], grant that we, who
> now joyfully receive Thine only-begotten Son as our
> Redeemer, may also, without fear, see coming as judge
> our Lord Jesus Christ...[PETITION]

Epiphany

> O God [DIRECT ADDRESS], who on this day, by the
> guiding of a star, didst reveal Thine only-begotten Son
> to the Gentiles [THEMATIC RELATIVE CLAUSE];
> mercifully grant, that we who now know Thee by faith,
> may be led on even to the contemplation of the beauty
> of Thy Majesty...[PETITION]

Pentecost

> O God [DIRECT ADDRESS], who on this day by the
> enlightening of the Holy Ghost didst teach the hearts
> of the faithful [THEMATIC RELATIVE CLAUSE]:
> grant us by the same Spirit to relish what is right, and
> ever to rejoice in His comfort...[PETITION]

The collect is formulaically intoned to a monotone with inflec-
tions. That it is intoned rather than "sung" helps to preserve its
corporate nature.

The Community listens to its story: Epistle, Gradual, Alleluia, Sequence, Gospel, Credo

---

We have heard with our ears, O God (Ps. 44: 1)

This section of the synaxis unfolds as a sequence of readings
with intervening chants of a highly lyrical nature, climaxing in

the verbal "entry" of Jesus, the reading of the Gospel. This entry is vividly underscored by the nature of the preceding chants (gradual, alleluia, and sequence) and by distinctive ceremonial that sets it apart.

Epistle and Gospel—Both the epistle and gospel are "intoned," recited largely on a monotone with various departures from the monotone to inflect the grammatical construction of the text. Thus commas, colons, question marks, and periods all bear musical analogies, as Example 6 below illustrates. This "singing" of the lessons does not comprise a "musical" event. Within the context of a sung liturgy, this type of intoning is largely the equivalent of reading the text aloud; it is didactically intended—a rational event. That it is sung at all owes much to the acoustical needs for audibility and the desire to solemnify the reading. But a reading it remains. And the minimal expressive possibilities of the monotone style promote an objective rendition—holy words "untainted" by the subjectivity of the reader/singer.

Example 6. Gospel intonation (Matthew 5:13; Common of Doctors)

following the *Liber Usualis* (Paris: Desclée, 1947)

The ceremonies surrounding the readings seek to establish a hierarchy between Epistle and Gospel, and in so doing, heighten the eventfulness of Christ's entry in the form of the Gospel reading. The epistle, for example, is sung to simpler

intonation formulas, and is sung by a subdeacon who receives
no special blessing prior to his reading. He holds the book of
Epistles for himself and has no special bidding for the people
who will hear the lesson. On the other hand, the Gospeller is a
deacon, ceremonially blessed by the celebrant in the liturgy to
commission his reading. The Gospel is carried in procession to
the place where it will be read with incense and candles, the
honorific trappings of the Roman empire now transferred to
Jesus' word. The subdeacon holds the Gospel book for the
deacon who, prior to reading, addresses the people with a bidding: "The Lord be with you." They in turn salute the Gospel
by framing it with "Glory to thee, Lord" or "Praise to thee,
Christ," as well as standing to hear it.

Where in the church the lessons were read is also distinctive. The ambo, the raised platform in basilical sanctuaries,
was the site of public reading. However, only the Gospel was
intoned from the platform itself; the epistle was read from the
steps to the ambo. Later in the Middle Ages, beginning by the
tenth century, the Gospel was read at the north of the sanctuary, while the epistle was read at the south. The north is mentioned variously in association with the devil or paganism,
both of which Christ confronts in the Gospels. [19]

Gradual and Alleluia—If the ceremonial itself builds climac-
tically to the reading of the Gospel, no less do the intervening
chants play a strong part in the unfolding of the drama. These
chants, responsorial in form, are effusive in their lyricism, rhapsodic in their nature, and somewhat complex in their function.
It is easy enough to hear in them a lyrical, affective response to

---

19. Concerning lesson ceremonies, see MRR 1: 403-419;
443-455 and A. Croegaert, *The Mass: A Liturgical
Commentary* (Westminster, Md.: The Newman Press,
1958), 1: 218-232.

the rational word—a manifestation of a balanced wholeness in the presence of God, with alternating "bi-camerality": rational lesson—affective response. And the notion of response is especially clear in earlier forms of the synaxis in which three lessons were read (Old Testament, Epistle, and Gospel), the first two each followed by a responsorial psalm. (Much traditional scholarship has linked the Christian practice of lessons with responsories to the synagogue. However, recent studies, especially those of James McKinnon and John A. Smith, challenge the traditional view, suggesting that psalmody in the synagogue arises only well into the Christian era, first documented as late as the eighth century.)[20] As in the rhythms we observed in chapter 2 governing the ebb and flow of office psalmody, i.e. contemplative recitation periodically taking flight in the lyric antiphon, so too does the "word" take flight in the lyricism of the responsorial psalm.[21]

The degree to which this was a lyric moment cannot be overstated. Most telling in this regard is that although the synaxis in the fifth or sixth century reduced its number of lessons from three to two, losing the Old Testament reading, it retained all of the intervening chants:

Earlier Pattern	*Later Pattern*
Old Testament	
resp. ps.	Epistle
Epistle	resp. ps. (Gradual)
resp. ps.	resp. ps. (Alleluia)
Gospel	Gospel

20. The traditional view is given voice by, among others, Croegaert, *Mass* 1: 204 and MRR 1: 422. The new view is articulated by McKinnon in "On the Question of Psalmody in the Ancient Synagogue," *Early Music History* 6 (1986): 159-191; and John A. Smith, "The Ancient Synagogue, the Early Church and Singing," *Music and Letters*, 65 (1984): 1–16.

The retention of, in essence, twice the song required by the function of interlude/response loudly bespeaks lyric priorities. The *music* was too good or too popular to let go. And with this high concentration of lyricism—a double dose—we perhaps see a second function emerge: not only is the responsorial chant an emotional outlet for what has come before, but it is also that which anticipates that which is to follow. Its now conspicuously lengthy lyric swell raises the affective pitch to a new level *for* the dramatic entry of Christ in the reading of the Gospel. As we will see below, this is further enhanced by the specifically transitional gestures of the sequence.

The responsorial style of both Gradual[22] and Alleluia features solo verses and choral responds. The use of soloists here is closely tied to the demands of the florid musical style, and, in the case of the graduals, a significant element of centoniza-

---

21. Cf. Jungmann: "It is in the very nature of things that the grace-laden message which God proclaims to men would awaken an echo of song. In the chant which is linked with the readings we have the most ancient song of the Christian Liturgy, and in particular of the Roman liturgy." MMR 1: 421. A similar circumstance may be seen in the Office in considering Matins responsories. Steiner cites: "To Mario Righetti, it seems that the responsories placed after each of the lessons of Matins may have either an esthetic role—that of providing articulation for the lessons, which if uninterrupted might become monotonous—or a dramatic one, enabling the congregation to express through prayer [song] the emotions experienced during the reading." "The Music for a Cluny Office," in *Monasticism and the Arts* (Syracuse: Syracuse University Press, 1984), 110, n.5. Steiner proposes that the interval between the lessons was a chance for reflection on the lessons, and that the responsory texts often seem chosen to promote this. (p. 82).

22. "Gradual" from the L. *gradus* = step, recalling its being sung from the steps of the ambo; the platform itself was reserved for the reading of the Gospel.

tion—construction by formula—that suggests an improvisa-
tional heritage. The degree of melisma here forms a voice of
rhapsody or ecstatic utterance.

The extended melisma on the "ia" of "alleluia" is appropriately styled the "jubilus," and it is difficult to veil the jubilation inherent in its tones. Augustine, in reference to jubilation
in the psalms is powerfully descriptive of joy beyond words
and, although he writes not of the alleluia jubilus itself, it is
difficult not to sense the resonance of his words with the mass
chant.

> Sing "in jubilation." For this is to sing well to God, to
> sing in jubilation. What is it to sing in jubilation? To be
> able to understand, to express in words, what is sung in
> the heart. For they who sing, either in the harvest, in
> the vineyard, or in some other arduous occupation, af-
> ter beginning to manifest their gladness in the words of
> songs, are filled with such joy that they cannot express
> it in words and turn from the syllables of words and
> proceed to the sound of jubilation. The jubilus is some-
> thing which signifies that the heart labors with what it
> cannot utter. And whom does jubilation befit but the
> ineffable God? For he is ineffable whom you cannot
> speak. And if you cannot speak him, yet ought not be
> silent, what remains but that you jubilate; so that the
> heart rejoices without words, and the great expanse of
> joy has not the limits of syllables?[23]

In a similar vein Augustine elsewhere observes that "One
who jubilates does not speak words, but is rather a sort of
sound of joy without words, since it is the voice of a soul
poured out in joy and expressing, as best it can, the feeling,
though not grasping the sense...."[24] Reaching out to the spe-

---

23. In Psalmum xxxii. MECL, 156.

cific context of the alleluia jubilus are Augustine's references to
God's ineffability. "Alleluia" (Hebrew "Hallelujah") means
"praise God," and the reference to God—"ia" or "jah", abbre-
viates the sacred *tetragrammaton*, YHWH or JHVH, the name
of God *too holy to speak aloud*. Thus, literally upon reaching
the name of God too holy to be named ("And if you cannot
speak him"...) the chant singer breaks into effusive melisma
("so that the heart rejoices without words"). The moment is
not only affectively rhapsodic, but also contemplatively rich,
as comments on both "jubilation" and the wordless dimension
suggest. For example, the fourteenth-century English mystic
and hermit, Richard Rolle, speaks of contemplative bliss as
"jubilation":

> To me it seems that contemplation is joyful song of
> God's love taken in mind, with sweetness of angels'
> praise. This is jubilation, that is the end of perfect
> prayer and high devotion in this life. This is that mirth
> in mind, had ghostly by the lover everlastingly, with
> great voice outbreaking...Nothing merrier than grace
> in contemplation.[25]

And the wordless rapture offers us the spiritual reward of an es-
cape from the "tyranny of words," seen by Jung as an impedi-
ment to recovering our "original feeling of unity."

> This rupture of the link with the unconscious and our
> submission to the tyranny of words have one great dis-
> advantage; the conscious mind becomes more and
> more the victim of its own discriminating activity, the
> picture we have of the world gets broken down into

24. In Psalmum xcix, MECL, 158.

25. In Heiler, "Contemplation in Christian Mysticism,"
228, 229.

countless particulars, and the original feeling of unity, which was integrally connected with the unity of the unconscious psyche, is lost.[26]

The responsorial chants then form a counterpose to the "rationality" of the lesson, rendered in, as we have seen, an objective, emotionally untainted intonation. Earlier we described the chant as an "affective response." Here we see it as much a "contemplative turning inward." The turn inward in melismatic chant is reinforced by many elements of Romanesque culture contemporary with the development of this style of chant. Spiralling manuscript illumination, exemplified in extreme forms by the Book of Kells or the Lindisfarne Gospels gives a compelling visual analogy not only to the spiraling contours of the sound of the chant, but also of the spiraling inwards of the soul. All were at home in a world view that favored the supernatural over the natural, as provocatively described by William Fleming:

> The Romanesque monk thus dwelt in a dream world where the trees that grew in Paradise, the angels who populated the heavens, and the demons of hell were more real than anything or anybody he beheld in everyday life. Even though he had never seen such creatures, he never doubted their existence. Indeed, the monsters whose fearsome characteristics were described in the bestiaries, and which were represented in the manuscripts and sculptures, had a moral and symbolic function far more real to him than any animals of mere physical existence. All these imaginary creatures existed together in a jungle of the imagination where the abnormal was the normal and the fabulous became the commonplace.[27]

---

26. Jung, "Transformation Symbols," 186.

So, in the interior world of the Romanesque spirit, the musical extremes of responsorial chant seem apt to illustrate the "abnormal" as "normal" and the "fabulous" as "commonplace."

To review, the lyric, soloistic style here serves several important functions:

1. to provide an affective response to the "rational" hearing of the scripture.
2. to build affective momentum for the hearing of the Gospel.
3. to accomplish a contemplative turning inward.

Significantly, though the particularities of musical style will vary, other renderings of the Gradual and Alleluia will preserve the same elements of rhapsody, floridity, and virtuosity, presumably to the same ends. And the most striking examples may be seen in the organal polyphony of the Notre Dame school. In the late twelfth and thirteenth centuries, Parisian composers like Leoninus and Perotinus brought forth innovative essays in the extension of musical space, rooted in the responsorial chants of the Proper. Their polyphonic settings graced high feasts, like Christmas, Easter, Pentecost, and Assumption; thus, not part of the daily liturgical practice, but rather a vocabulary of embellishment dictated by the hierarchy of the church calendar. Music, as we observed earlier, is but one of many ways in which the calendar was inflected. Craig Wright enumerates the variety of ways this was true at Notre Dame:

> This rigidly hierarchical application of polyphony to the liturgy is fully consonant with other regulations governing the celebration of the divine offices at the cathedral: the number of candles, the number of soloists,

27. William Fleming, *Arts and Ideas* (New York: Holt, Rinehart and Winston, 1986), 130.

the splendor of the copes, and even the closeness of the
shave on the face and tonsure of the clergy of the
church were a direct reflection of the rank of the day.[28]

(Other places and times promote the same idea. For example,
the antiphonal music so strongly associated with the Basilica of
St. Mark's in Venice in the late sixteenth century was also occasioned by considerations of the calendar, in particular those
days when the gold altar piece, the *pala d'oro*, was opened.)[29]
   Modern descriptions of the Notre Dame repertory underscore its soloistic virtuosity: "a virtuoso art, a tour de force for
composer and performer alike"; an attempt to "capture and
recast what was at heart a virtuosic, linear vocal style, one
heavily dependent on improvisatory technique."[30] Leoninus'
well-known Easter alleluia, "Pascha nostrum," illustrates the
continuity from the chant of the florid, rhapsodic style, har-
nessed for the same ends of nearly wordless effusion. The linear extension of musical space here—that is, the long
prolongation of the cantus firmus—also underscores the
"abnormal" become "normal" and the "irrational" arresting of
any perceptible progress through "rational" verbal space. The
nature of the polyphonic duplum here seems also to suggest
the spiraling gestures of the turn inward.[31]   The degree of
stylistic correspondence between the responsorial chants and
the Notre Dame organal settings of them is significant in its
own right: the chant as an elongated cantus firmus is robbed of

28. See Craig Wright, *Music and Ceremony*, 266.

29. See Iain Fenlon, *Music and Society: The Renaissance*
(Englewood Cliffs, N.J.: Prentice-Hall, 1989), 114-115.

30. Edward Roesner, "The Performance of Parisian
Organum," *Early Music* 7 (1979): 174. Roesner also
addresses singing *in floratura*, in which the already florid
line is subjected to performer-added embellishment. See
also Wright, *Music and Ceremony*, 289.

its life; thus its particular values (floridity, rhapsody, etc.) are transferred and preserved in the polyphony, because the *liturgical function* of the gradual/alleluia requires them.

Sequence—In the ninth through the twelfth centuries, the Sequence arose as a regional embellishment of the juncture between Alleluia and Gospel. Some evidence suggests that the early Sequence was, in part, the result of textual troping of the alleluia jubilus, as related by the ninth-century monk Notker Balbulus.[32] Other early sequences as well as maturer examples are independent in origin. A large and popular repertory—ca. 4500 survive[33]—the Sequence functions to provide transition from Alleluia to the Gospel and, in their emotive range within single pieces, they may also be seen to be "transitional songs" between different emotive states. Nancy van Deusen has treat-

31. "Pascha nostrum" is excerpted in the *Norton Anthology of Western Music* (New York: W.W. Norton, 1988),1: 47. The intricacy of repetition of detail in this style—small cells continually repeated, for example—remind of Jungmann's observations concerning Gothic cumulation, wherein the repetition of ornament or detail parallels the proliferation of liturgical detail, such as kissing the altar, a ceremonial detail that in the thirteenth-century was done every time the celebrant turned around at the altar. MMR 1: 107.

32. See Richard Crocker, *The Early Medieval Sequence* (Berkeley: University of California Press, 1977). Crocker's work deals with the Notkerian sequence. For a recent study of the late sequence, see Margot Elsbeth Fassler, *Gothic Song: Victorine sequences and Augustinian reform in twelfth-century Paris* (Cambridge: Cambridge University Press, 1993).

33. Of the large number employed regionally, only four survived the Council of Trent which legislated as standard Victimae Paschali Laudes (Easter), Lauda Sion (Corpus Christi), Veni Sancte Spiritus (Pentecost), and Dies Irae (Requiem). Stabat Mater was added in the 18th century.

ed this transitional function at length.[34] To her, the Old Testament world of the psalmic Alleluia and the New Testament world of the Gospel reading is given a bridge in the Sequence, a bridge resonant with psalm commentaries which sought the same connection. Van Deusen writes:

> This transition between the Old Testament—the alleluia with its psalmodic verse, and the New Testament Gospel reading—is made by the sequence. It is a genre based on transition, neither arbitrary nor accidental. There is an internal logic for just this type at just this place, serving a specific function in the organization of the mass ceremony. The central themes recurring in sequence texts are just those which have roots in the OT, and resolution and clarification in the NT. These themes include the prophets and their prediction linked to Christ..., the serpent and Eve related to Mary..., the creation and the "God-man"..., David with Christ..., the Law of Moses with the inner "Law" of grace..., OT heroes of faith united with the saints by Christ's sacrifice..., and the synagogue consolidated with the ecclesia or Christian believers.[35]

Moreover, the bridge is not only a textual one, but a musical one as well. This is easily seen in the progressive verbalization of the style: the melismatic alleluia gives way to the spare reci-

---

34. See Nancy van Deusen, in "The Use and Significance of Sequence" in *The Harp and the Soul* (Lewiston, N.Y.: Edwin Mellen Press, 1989), 109-164.

35. van Deusen, *Harp and Soul,* 114.

tation of the Gospel reading through the *syllabic* chant of the sequence:

MUSIC

Alleluia	Sequence	Gospel
Melismatic	syllabic	recitational

WORD

Credo—The Credo on Sundays and other feasts brings the synaxis to a conclusion with an affirmation of the tenets of the faith, an affirmation that also responds to the instruction that has preceded; in a sense, a corporate "we have heard, and this is what we take it to be." (The corporate nature is challenged by the first person singular of "Credo"—*I* believe—but this derives from the earlier use of the creed in the baptismal rite by the individual catechumens.) The text, known as the Nicene Creed, is Trinitarian in form and based on the work of two fourth-century Church councils: Nicea and Constantinople. Although the Trinity is based on co-equality of Persons, the text swells in reference to the Son, while the Father and the Holy Spirit are dealt with in less expansive terms. Ritual gesture and music respond in kind. For example, at the text of the incarnation (*et incarnatus est de Spiritu Sancto ex Maria Virgine: et homo factus est.* He came down from heaven, took flesh of the Virgin Mary by the action of the Holy Spirit, and was made man) the recounting of the miracle is haloed by genuflection (since the eleventh century or earlier).[36] This posture of reverence is frequently echoed in polyphonic settings of the Creed, as the following passage from Machaut's *Mass of Notre Dame* (Example 7 on page 103-104) shows.

---

36. MRR 1: 466.

Example 7. Guillaume de Machaut *Mass of Notre Dame*. "Credo" (mm. 59–79).

Guillaume de Machaut, *Musikalische Werke*, ed. by Heinrich Besseler (Leipzig: Breitkopf & Härtel, [n.d.]), 4: 9, Used by permission.

Similar examples appear in the *Missa Pange Lingua* by Josquin and the *Mass in g-minor* by Vaughan Williams and many others. The musical gesture is generally a slow, chordal passage in contrast to its surroundings.

THE EUCHARIST

The community offers gifts of bread and wine: the Offertory

Ascribe to the Lord the honor due his Name; bring offerings and come into his courts. (Ps 96:8)

Offertory—The second part of the mass, the Eucharist, sacramentally enacts the mystery of Jesus' presence in communion. This sacramental part of the liturgy is ushered in by the offertory. The offertory functions on several levels:

1. Bread and wine are offered that there may be material substance to consecrate. That the material is bread and wine follows Jesus' model from Maundy Thursday: "Then he took a cup... Then he took a loaf of bread." That the bread and wine will become His body and blood, broken and offered in sacrifice, and that the bread and wine are the gifts *of* the community bring a sharp focus to the community's identification with the sacrificed, i.e. the community *as* the body of Christ.[37] And significantly, this identification—the community as the body—is a key to understanding the eucharistic ritual as a transformative rite. As the bread and wine are transformed into the sacred ele-

---

37. Cf. SL, 117-18: "The offertory in the original view of the rite is therefore something much more than a ceremonial action, the placing of bread and wine upon the altar by the clergy as an inevitable preparation for communion. It is as the later liturgies continued to call it... the "rational worship" by free reasonable creatures of their Creator, a self-sacrificial act by which each Christian comes to his being as a member of Christ in the 're-calling' before God of the self-sacrificial offering of Christ on Calvary. 'There you are upon the table.,' says Augustine...'there you are in the chalice.'"

ments of Body and Blood, so too the community is transformed—*as* the Body and *into* the Body.

2. Gifts of diverse kinds (at various times not only bread and wine) are offered as a ritual oblation and for the support of the community, especially the clergy. Bread and wine *are* the standard gifts, and that not used at the altar could be used domestically by the clergy and the poor. However, the change from the use of leavened bread to unleavened bread taking place between the seventh and eleventh centuries[38] would naturally render this impossible. Gifts of the faithful would eventually take the form of mass stipends, i.e. payment for a private mass offered on their behalf.[39]

3. The offering of bread and wine introduces a rich vocabulary of symbols into the rite. Some of the symbolism is very direct and particular, such as the medieval affinity for red wine in the chalice to evoke the color of blood.[40] Others require more interpretation. For example, the composite nature of the elements of bread and wine—bread from diverse grains, wine from many grapes—symbolizes the unity of the church composed of the diverse faithful. And, where the bread is present in the form of the unleavened Host, its disc shape dramatically becomes a mandala of wholeness in which all parts are integrated into the one containing circle.

Some symbolic readings reclaim earlier "neutral" practices. For example, in the ancient world, wine was customarily mixed with water, a practice echoed in the offertory's preparation of the chalice: the cup receives both wine and water. And though it may be attributed to custom, it is prone to symbolical interpretation as well, namely it suggests Christ's mixed nature: fully human (water) and fully divine (wine). Others

---

38. See Croegaert, *Mass*, 2: 85.

39. Klauser, *Short History*, 110.

40. Croegaert, *Mass*, 2: 86.

have suggested that, in that once mixed the wine and water cannot be separated, it evokes the unity of Christ (wine) and his Church (water).[41] In either case it is significant that the symbolic content emerges out of an already existing practice. Many symbols seem to arise this way, especially after their practicality has become moot. To this point Eric Hobsbawm observes:

> [O]bjects or practices are liberated for full symbolic and ritual use when no longer fettered by practical use. The spurs of Cavalry officers' dress uniforms are more important for 'tradition' when there are no horses...the wigs of lawyers could hardly acquire their modern significance until other people stopped wearing wigs.[42]

Thus, the mixture of water and wine begins as social custom, but becomes symbolic, like the officer's spurs. The same point can also be tellingly made about much liturgical vesture.

Other symbolic readings arise out of the ceremonial of the offertory as opposed to the offering itself. For example, in preparing the Host, it is elevated—raised honorifically towards the altar cross. In so doing, as Jung has observed, one symbolically associates the offering with the bodily sacrifice on the cross and one also "elevates" the bread from the sphere of the material to that of the spiritual.[43]

The offertory could be a lengthy action, especially as its early form featured a procession to the altar by all members of

---

41. See Jung, "Transformation Symbols," 105; Croegaert, *Mass*, 2: 96-97.

42. Eric Hobsbawm, "Introduction: Inventing Traditions," in *The Invention of Tradition* (Cambridge: Cambridge University Press, 1984), 4.

43. See Jung, "Transformation Symbols," 104.

the congregation bearing gifts. The first Roman Ordo (eighth century) describes the offertory rite of a papal liturgy which, though curtailing the participation of the congregation, was an elaborate affair indeed. The ceremony detailed below required the liturgical cover of the offertory chant:

> The pontiff now goes down to the place where the notables sit,… and he receives the loaves of the princes… The archdeacon next receives the flasks of wine, and pours them into the greater chalice…A district-subdeacon takes the a linen cloth held by two collets. An hebdomadary bishop receives the rest of the loaves after the pontiff, so that he may, with his own hand, put them into the linen cloth which is carried after him. Following him the deacon-attendant receives the flasks of wine and pours them into the bowl with his own hand, after the archdeacon. Meanwhile the pontiff, before passing over to the women's side, goes down before the Confession, and there receives the loaves of the chancellor, the secretary, and the chief counsellor…In like manner the pontiff goes up to the women's side, and performs there all things in the same order as detailed above. And the presbyters do likewise, should there be need, either after the pontiff or in the presbytery.
>
> After this, the pontiff returns to his throne…, and there washes his hands. The archdeacon stands before the altar and washes his hands at the end of the collection of the offerings. Then he looks the pontiff in the face, signs to him, and, after the pontiff has returned his salutation, approaches the altar.
>
> Then the district-subdeacons, taking the loaves from the hand of the subdeacon-attendant, and carrying them in their arms, bring them to the archdeacon, who arranges them on the altar. The subdeacons, by the bye, bring up the loaves on either side. Having made

the altar ready, the archdeacon then takes the pontiff's flask of wine from the subdeacon-oblationer, and pours it through a strainer into the chalice; then the deacons' flasks...as well. Then the subdeacon-attendant goes down into the choir, receives a ewer of water from the hand of the ruler of the choir and brings it back to the archdeacon, who pours it into the chalice, making a cross as he does so. Then the deacons go up to the pontiff...

Then the pontiff, arising from his throne, goes down to the altar and salutes it, and receives the loaves from the hands of the hebdomadary presbyter and the deacons. Then the archdeacon receives the pontiff's loaves from the subdeacon-oblationer, and gives them to the pontiff. And when the latter had placed them on the altar, the archdeacon takes the chalice from the hand of a district-subdeacon and sets it on the altar on the right side of the pontiff's loaf.... Then he lays the veil on the end of the altar, and stands behind the pontiff, and the latter bows slightly to the altar and then turns to the choir and signs to them to stop singing.[44]

For this elaborate, hierarchical ceremony, psalmody, as with the introit, provided a variable length musical accompaniment. Paralleling the introit, whose action—and accordingly whose music as well—was drastically abbreviated, the offertory too loses its congregational and processional nature, and its need for variable length accompaniment. In the eleventh century, the offertory chant becomes only an antiphon, with no psalm verses at all.[45] However, truncated or no, as a *choral* chant, it continues to assert the corporate nature of the offer-

44. *Ordo Romanus Primus,* pp. 133-137.

45. See Croegaert, *Mass* 2: 74 et seq. and MRR, 2: 7 et seq. for detailed discussion.

tory action, even though it had become, in the main, reserved to clerics.

The community, through the action of the priest, blesses the bread and wine. Preface, Sanctus-Benedictus, Canon, Pater Noster

---

You spread a table before me… (Ps. 23:5)

Preface, Sanctus–Benedictus—One of the most mystically thrilling texts in Hebrew scripture recounts the vision of God in glory by the prophet Isaiah:

> In the year that King Uzziah died, I saw the Lord sitting on a throne, high and lofty; and the hem of his robe filled the temple. Seraphs were in attendance above him; each had six wings: with two they covered their faces, and with two they covered their feet, and with two they flew. And one called to another and said:
>
> 'Holy, holy, holy is the Lord of hosts;
> the whole earth is full of his glory.'
>
> The pivots on the thresholds shook at the voices of those who called, and the house filled with smoke.

This antiphonal song of the angelic orders amid the wafting clouds of incense in the heavenly temple is traditionally held to be ceaseless song, unending praise. And, in the mass, as temporal bounds dissolve, the "earthly choir" enters momentarily into this eternal chant[46] of heaven in the singing of the Sanctus. The celestial Sanctus is perpetual, the terrestial limited, though the two briefly merge—become synchronized—at this point of the Mass.

Many have given voice to the notion of earthly and heavenly choirs uniting in the Sanctus. St. Clement of Rome (fl. ca. 96), for instance, suggests in his First Epistle to the Corinthians:

Let us consider the entire multitude of his angels, how standing by you they minister to his will. For the Scripture says: 'Ten thousand times ten thousand stood by him and a thousand times a thousand ministered to him and cried out, "Holy, holy, holy is the Lord of Sabaoth, the whole of creation is full of his glory." ' Let us, therefore, gathered together in concord by conscience, cry out earnestly to him as if with one voice, so that we might come to share in his great and glorious promises.[47]

---

46. Vicktor Zuckerkandl, in his provocative *Sound and Symbol: Music and the External World* (New York: Pantheon Books, 1951) notes the seemingly inherent contradiction between chant (music as measured time) and eternity (beyond time). He writes: "A God enthroned beyond time in timeless eternity would have to renounce music. The visible world in the fullness of its beauty lies spread out before the spatial omnipresence of God; but temporal omnipresence would make the revelation of audible beauty impossible. It argues against God's timelessness. Are we to suppose that we mortals, in possessing such a wonder as music, are more privileged than God? Rather, to save music for Him, we shall hold, with the Greeks, that God cannot go beyond time. Otherwise what would He be doing with all the choiring angels?" (p. 151)

47. MECL, 18. On this same point, see J. D. Crichton, "A Theology of Worship," in *The Study of Liturgy*, 18.

Example 8. *Sursum corda* (Tonus ferialis)

Following the *Liber Usualis* (Paris: Desclée, 1947)

V   The Lord be with you.
R   And with thy spirit
V   Lift up your hearts
R   We lift them up unto the Lord
V   Let us give thanks unto our Lord God.
R   It is meet and right so to do.

The drama of entering into the "eternal" Sanctus is well prepared by the dialogue of the *Sursum corda* and the Preface
which immediately follows it. The *Sursum corda* (Example 8
above) is a preparatory bidding in which the celebrant invites
the community to "lift up their hearts" and to offer thanks to
God. In other words, they are summoned to participate in the
eucharistic action now about to get underway. The dialogue between celebrant and people, or later their surrogate, the choir,
introduces an element of response and gathering together that
is significant in several ways. (1) As a dialogue, it gathers the
disparate voices of celebrant and people together so that they
may be harmonized in the unified song of the Sanctus, which
itself binds together earth and heaven. (2) Tellingly, the third
response of the dialogue—"It is meet and right so to do"—gives
also the consent of the group to the sacrificial action of the individual celebrant which follows. All take part in the dialogue;
all permit the priest to act on their behalf.[48] (3) The dialogue

form itself loosely suggests or foreshadows the angelic antiphony of the Sanctus in which one angel sings to another. (4) But,
at its most basic level, the dialogue reminds us that the liturgy
itself is a *response* to God; here a notable marriage of form and
essence.[49]

The notion of dialogue, antiphony and response can be
reinforced by the reverberant acoustic of many churches. For
example, Keith Critchlow writes of the Gothic span at Char-
tres:

> The height above the ground has to do with the delayed
> action of the voice going out and coming back... So the
> whole experience of the chanting rising to the vaulting
> and returning or coming back down is like the angels
> replying to you and yet of course it is yourself.[50]

The Preface which emerges out of the Sursum corda
accomplishes essentially two things. One is to particularize the
feast with reference to important themes of the day or season,
as the examples below suggest:

Proper Preface for Easter

> But chiefly are we bound to praise thee for the glo-
> rious resurrection of thy Son Jesus Christ our
> Lord; for he is the very Paschal Lamb, who was sac-
> rificed for us, and hath taken away the sins of the
> world; who by his death hath destroyed death, and

---

48. Marion Hatchett, *Commentary on the American Prayer
Book* (New York: Seabury Press, 1980), 361.

49. Cf. Crichton: "Because it is God who always takes the
initiative, Christian worship is best discussed in terms of
response. In worship we respond to God." "A Theology of
Worship," 9.

50. See *Parabola*, 34.

by his rising to life again hath won for us everlasting life.

Proper Preface for Ascension

Through thy dearly beloved Son Jesus Christ our
Lord; who after his glorious resurrection manifest-
ly appeared to his disciples; and in their sight as-
cended into heaven, to prepare a place for us; that
where he is, there we might also be, and reign with
him in glory.

And having particularized the occasion, the Preface makes explicit that the song to be sung unites with that of heaven:

*Therefore with Angels and Archangels, and with all
the company of heaven,* we laud and magnify thy
glorious Name; evermore praising thee, and saying: SANCTUS...

This explicit reference in the text is sometimes reinforced
by music that evokes the traditions of angelic song in programmatic gestures. In general, the imitative style of the high
Renaissance was well suited to mirror angelic antiphony, as
one voice "cries to another" in succession. In Lasso's *Missa Bell'
Amfitri* (Example 9 on page 115) it takes little imagination to
hear the angels' characteristic dialogue in the passing of imitative material from one part to another. However, as this imitative style was so pervasive, its potential programmatic
associations were neutralized. And one must go to extremes to
convey the program. Josquin, for example, in his Missa Pange
Lingua writes his Benedictus in a strikingly unusual fashion.
Antiphonal phrases proceed without *any* contrapuntal overlap,
a device that allows the listener to bracket the phrases outside
the usual imitative syntax and give them associative meaning.
Other angel pieces similarly had to resort to extremes of different sorts. Ockeghem's thirty-six-voice canon on Deo Gratias
may evoke the sounds of the celestial hierarchy in its vast

antiphonal scoring.[51] Also unusually scored to similar ends is Robert Wylkinson's "Salve Regina" in the Eton Choirbook.

In our century, programmatic antiphony in the Sanctus persists, as seen for example in the gently wafting undulation of Vaughan Williams' Sanctus in his Mass in g-minor or the cumulative chain of seraphic trumpetings in Stravinsky's Mass.

Example 9. Orlando di Lasso *Missa Bell'Amfitri* "Sanctus" (mm. 1–4)

Orland de Lassus, *Sämtliche Werke neue Reihe*, ed. by Siegfried Hermelink (Kassel: Bärenreiter, 1968), 8: 83. Used by permission.

51. See Edward Lowinsky, "Ockeghem's Canon for Thirty-Six Voices: an Essay in Music Iconography," in *Essays in Musicology in honor of Dragan Plamenac* (Pittsburgh: University of Pittsburgh Press, 1969): 155-180.

It is significant as well that the Sanctus does not "just begin." The *Sursum corda* and Preface build a rhetorical momentum which *climaxes* in the Sanctus, affording it a heightened sense of drama, a reverential entry of the song.

Canon—The canon (or eucharistic prayer) is that prayer in which the sacrifice is offered to God and through which the offered elements of bread and wine are sacramentally transubstantiated into the sacred elements of Christ's body and blood. Several prayers and texts are woven together to comprise the traditional canon of the Roman Rite. In outline form[52] it proceeds as follows:

> • prayer that the gifts offered will be acceptable and blessed

> • prayer of particular intention (i.e. the mass may be offered on behalf of those named here)

> • Reverencing of the Blessed Virgin Mary and apostles and martyrs

> • Prayer that the offering may become the body and blood of Jesus

> • Consecration of the host, using the words of Jesus at the Last Supper of Maundy Thursday: "Take, all of you, and eat of this, for this is my body."

> • The host is elevated at this point for all to adore

> • Consecration of the wine, again using the words of Jesus from Maundy Thursday: 'Take, all of you, and drink of this, for this is the chalice of my blood of the new and everlasting cov-

---

52. Following the *Missale Romanum* transcribed in Thompson, *Liturgies of the Western Church*, 72-77.

enant, a mystery of faith. It shall be shed for you and many others, so that sins may be forgiven.' The chalice is elevated

• Prayer to accept the offering

• Prayer that God's holy angel will carry the sacrifice to the heavenly altar, and in turn that those who partake of the Body and Blood may be filled with spiritual grace and blessing.

• Memorial of the dead

• Prayer that those offering the sacrifice may find a place in the fellowship of the holy apostles and martyrs.

The focus is, of course, on the consecration itself, authoritatively rooted in Jesus' words of institution. And although it is a particular consecration, offered by particular people in a particular place at a particular time, the references to the communion of saints and the heavenly altar bring to the particular a rich context of catholicity and timelessness (the same bridging of the temporal and timeless perceived in the singing of the Sanctus).

The canon is at the heart of the sacramental mystery. As a gesture of respect, in the eighth century the canon was recited inaudibly—holiest of words spoken in hushed, reverential tones. And though proceeding out of respect, it also had the effect of privatizing the sacramental action. As Jungmann describes it, the canon was a "sanctuary which only the priest could enter," a verbal holy of holies. A visual holy of holies as well, for at this time the celebrant, as general practice, faced east, thus hiding the sacred action from a distant congregation with his body. Ironically, the celebrant's position facing east, in front of the altar, which shields some of the liturgical actions from view may proceed originally from the desire to make other things visible. Dix cites, for instance, that the Western interest in viewing brought the reliquaries up from under the altars onto the altars and later, on pedestals behind the altar, forcing the celebrant to move to the front.[53]

The inaudible canon, as mentioned in chapter 2, was recited *while* the Sanctus continued being sung by the choir. This is, in part, an interesting renunciation of rational, linear time in favor of mysterious or "heavenly" atemporality. But also, one suspects, it is partially related to the expansion of the musical content of the Sanctus. In other words, were the celebrant required to wait for the Sanctus to conclude before beginning the canon, one could easily imagine how this would deter the expansion of the music.

Dramatically underscoring the mystery and awe of the consecration is the practice of elevation, chiefly of the host. (Elevation of the chalice becomes fully established only in the later sixteenth century.)[54] The practice of raising the host above the priest's head so that it may be seen and adored— venerated with genuflections, incense, and bells—and in being seen impart a particular grace to the beholder, emerges in Paris in the late twelfth century. At that time, debate was concerned with specifying at what point in the canon the consecration was complete, i.e. when did Christ become present in the species? The elevation of the Host after the first words of institution—"for this is my body"—ritually and emphatically emphasized the view that Christ was fully present in the Host at that point, not requiring the consecration of the chalice to render Him "complete." [55] This liturgical innovation was not only a vivid signpost in the evolution of the nature of the mass (the holy meal of the faithful transformed into an objective adoration), but also a popular focus for the faithful, progressively disenfranchised from the altar. This, "the most signifi-

53. See SL, 591.

54. MRR, 2: 208.

cant ceremonial development in the West"[56] became not only central to mass piety, but in some cases the sum of it. Bishop Hope records:

> The high point of this tremendous and intense drama of the Holy Sacrifice was the moment of elevation of the sacred host just after the consecration; indeed to view the host became at times the sole object of Mass devotion. Folk went from church to church in order to see this moment as often as they could, often rushing in just before and leaving as hurriedly as they had come.[57]

Those who had once partaken of the bread of heaven as spiritual sustenance now gazed from afar, not at heavenly manna but at God enthroned. It is historically significant that this change, in a sense, marks both a rise in (masculine) clericalism and a repression of the traditionally feminine associations of feeding. Caroline Walker Bynum's landmark study, *Holy Feasts and Holy Fasts* suggests that the affinity between food and female is a strong one, proceeding from various quarters, including that food is generally a "woman-controlled resource" (both domestically and biologically), that through food women control themselves and those around them, and that women have been given to symbolize the physical and the material.[58] That the "female" feeding (mass as a holy meal) is

55. See, *inter alia*, the contextually rich account of this development in Caroline Walker Bynum's *Holy Feast and Holy Fast: the Religious Significance of Food to Medieval Women* (Berkeley: University of California Press, 1987), 48 et seq.

56. Hugh Wybrew, "The Setting of the Liturgy: Ceremonial," in the *Study of Liturgy,* 489.

57. D.M Hope, "Medieval Western Rites," 282.

replaced by an objectified presence to look at (the elevated host) may also be seen to conform to certain gender constructions in which woman is objectified in order that she may be looked upon.[59]

This late Medieval twist locates the high point in a visual experience. But, to state the obvious, it is a visual experience that derives its considerable affective power from its context: the small white host, in and of itself, is not much to look at, and its spiritual identity is a mystery unseen by the eyes. However, gesture, liturgical context, visual setting, smell, and in a large way, sound, combine to give the moment a dramatically sustainable, affective impact. (This reliance on a number of factors or senses finds an analogy in the medieval feast. Caroline Walker Bynum observes, "As culinary historians have recently observed, the characteristic medieval meal was the feast, and it was more an aesthetic and social event than a gastronomic one. The feast was a banquet for all the senses; indeed, food was almost an excuse for indulging senses other than taste.")[60] Music for the elevation was not only popular, as we will see below, but it was an important factor in shaping the nature of the action. Never more so, perhaps, than in the seventeenth century.

Following the Roman *Caeremoniale* of 1606, we see the delaying of the singing of the polyphonic Benedictus until the elevation of the Host. Thus the polyphonic Sanctus would enclose the first part of the canon; the benedictus would cover

58. Bynum, *Holy Feast*, 189, 193, 262, 270, *inter alia*.

59. See for example John Berger's *Ways of Seeing* (Harmondsworth, Eng.: Penguin Books, 1972) or Gill Saunders' *The Nude: a New Perspective* (New York: Harper Collins, 1989).

60. See Bynum, *Holy Feast*, 60.

and enrich the elevation. Significantly however, for it documents the degree to which music figured in the elevation, the
benedictus was replaceable by instrumental music for the elevation. Instrumental music in the seventeenth century was
used in several places of the liturgy—in addition to the elevation, the gradual, offertory, and communion invited this treatment. And composers would often associate particular forms
or styles with particular liturgical functions (canzonas for the
gradual, communion, and Deo Gratias; ricercars for the Offertory; slow, chromatic pieces for the Elevation).[61] It is historically significant that this comes into prominence in the early
seventeenth century, for it thus coincides with the emergence
of instrumental music as an idiomatically independent style.
However, regardless of its degree of stylistic independence, like
liturgical vocal music, it remains here tied to a particular,
extra-musical function. Stylistic independence from vocal
musical styles closely tied to social function did not move
instrumental music away from the social function; only away
from the particularities of the style itself.

Unsurprisingly, given the taste of the time, instrumental
music was popular in the liturgy. In 1623, Ignazio Donati tellingly observes:

> the Sanctus and Agnus Dei are placed so simply and
> briefly in the Venetian style to hurry them up and to

61. See Stephen Bonta, "The Uses of the Sonata da
Chiesa," *Journal of the American Musicological Society,* 22
(1969): 54–84, esp. 71, 75. See also Anne Schnoebelen,
"The Role of the Violin in the resurgence of the Mass in the
17th century," *Early Music,* 18 (1990): 537-542, and James
H. Moore, "The Liturgical Use of the Organ in
Seventeenth-Century Italy: New Documents, New
Hypotheses," in *Frescobaldi Studies* (Durham: Duke
University Press, 1987): 351-383.

give place to the Concerto for the Elevation and to some Sinfonie at the Communion.[62]

Little mistaking the priorities there.

Girolamo Frescobaldi offers several examples of elevation toccatas in both his *Second Book of Toccatas, Canzonas...* (1637) and the *Fiori Musicali* (1635). They favor chromaticism, frequent use of harmonic sevenths, a high degree of affectivity, and a "wandering" style. All of these traits combine to give a mystical aura to the event, enclosing it in an ineffable sonic cloud of incense. The harmonic surprises resist a rational grounding; the chromatic turns, often surprising, undermine firm footing; the wandering of both melody and harmony denies easily perceived linear goals, prompting Frederick Hammond to observe here "the sensation of timeless contemplation... the musical creation of a kind of eternal present."[63] These mystical touches are further underscored by mode. The elevation toccatas of the *Fiori Musicali* are all three in e-mode, which, in some sixteenth-century theory was associated with the "unspeakable."[64] The chromaticism too tinges the whole with a sweet sadness, evoking the sacrifice of Golgotha out of whose shadow the present moment of transcendence arises.

In more detail, the "toccata cromaticha" from *Fiori Musicali* exemplifies well the extent of Frescobaldi's use of chromaticism at the elevation, encompassing both straightforward chromatic melody to evoke affectively Christ's passion (Exam-

---

62. In Schnoebelen, "Role of the Violin," 538.

63. Frederick Hammond, *Girolamo Frescobaldi* (Cambridge: Harvard University Press, 1983), 182-183.

64. See Willi Apel, The *History of Keyboard Music to 1700* (Bloomington: Indiana University Press, 1972), 478.

ple 10 below) and chromatic alteration that leads to rationally unexpected places in its somewhat wrenching progression to the next harmonic pillar (Example 11 below).

Example 10. Girolamo Frescobaldi *Toccata chromaticha* (mm. 25–27)

Girolamo Frescobaldi, *Orgel- und Klavierwerke*, ed. by Pierre Pidoux (Kassel: Bärenreiter, 1963), 5: 18. Used by permission.

Example 11. Girolamo Frescobaldi *Toccata chromaticha* (mm. 1–7)

Girolamo Frescobaldi, *Orgel- und Klavierwerke*, ed. by Pierre Pidoux (Kassel: Bärenreiter, 1963), 5: 18. Used by permission.

The chromaticism and modulatory nature of this passage and others like it suggest that instead of chords "moving" one to another, the sonorities are rather "transformed" into new ones. The harmonic richness may evoke the irrational or mystical, but it is the transformative[65] that most lingers, entering into the transformation of those who view the sacrament and the transformation of the bread into the Body of Christ.

Example 12. Girolamo Frescobaldi *Toccata* (mm. 31–33).

Girolamo Frescobaldi, *Orgel und Klavierwerke*, ed. by Pierre Pidoux (Kassel: Bärenreiter, 1963), 5: 43 Used by permission

Example 13. Alessandro Grandi *O quam tu pulchra es, Ghirlando sacra, Libro primo* (Venice, 1675)

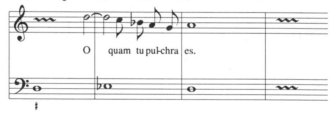

That the sight of the sacrament is sweet is rapturously underscored in passages like Example 12 above from another elevation toccata in *Fiori Musicali*. Here the sweet dissonance of the major seventh on the third beat of the second measure is highly sensual and is given a more explicit meaning when heard with texts like "O Quam tu pulchra es" (O how fair you are) set by Alessandro Grandi (Example 13 above).

The Lord's Prayer follows the Eucharistic Prayer, and its recitation looks ahead to the communion to follow: (1) in its petition "give us today our daily bread" the bread of the altar,

65. Cf. Apel, *Keyboard Music*, 470-471 where Apel links bold modulation and mystical transformation.

the body of Christ, is foreshadowed; and (2) with its plea for forgiveness, it brings one to communion "confessed."[66]

The bread is broken and shared: Fraction, Agnus Dei, and Communion

---

So mortals ate the bread of angels (Ps 78: 24)

Fraction and Agnus Dei—The breaking of leavened bread for the worshipping community—the fraction—is a liturgical action that was potentially time-consuming and requiring variable length musical cover. With the seventh century at Rome, this took the form of the Agnus Dei, a text which underscores the identification of Jesus with the sacrifice of the altar in context of a Paschal victim:

> O Lamb of God who takes away the sin of the world, have mercy upon us.

As cover for the action, this verse could be infinitely repeated. However, with the infrequency of laical communion (rare after the fifth century, except in Rome)[67] and the use of unleavened bread, the fraction is, if not less eventful, less time consuming and the Agnus text is truncated to three repetitions, the last ending not with the plea for mercy, but rather an imploration for God's peace.[68]

---

66. MRR 2: 276-7, 283. Cf. the traditional practice of pre-Eucharistic confession and fasting practices which reflect the Pauline admonition of 1 Cor. 11: 27-29.

67. SL, 598.

68. MRR 2: 332-339.

Communion—The Communion chant, like the introit and offertory, is music tied to action, in this case the act of ritually eating the bread and wine. And in parallel course to the other chants, it too became truncated as the action required: here, as in the offertory, only an antiphon remains.

Psalm singing during the communion can be traced back to the fourth century; the earliest reference is possibly from Cyril of Jerusalem:

> After these things, listen to the singer who invites us with a sacred melody to communion in the holy mysteries, and says: 'Taste and see that the Lord is good' (Ps. 34: 9)[69]

The use of psalm 34 is natural in its topical reference. Many antiphons share this close topicality, especially those drawn from Gospel texts. For example, on Epiphany II the Communion antiphon reprises some of the Gospel of the day concerning Jesus' wine miracle at the wedding in Cana.

> Jesus said to them, "Fill the jars with water...and take it to the chief steward.... When the steward tasted the water that had become wine,...[he] said to [the bridegroom]...You have kept the good wine until now." Jesus did this, the first of his signs....(John 2: 7-11)

Obviously the reference to wine and transformation are contextually rich here. Other communions strike a similar tone, such as the following from Lenten Thursdays:

> (Thursday after Lent I)

> The bread that I will give for the life of the world is my flesh. (John 6:51)

> (Thursday after Lent II)

---

69. MECL, 76-77.

> Those who eat my flesh and drink my blood abide
> in me, and I in them. (John 6: 56)

Others forsake reference to the action in favor of reinforcing
the liturgical theme of the day, especially on major feasts.

The Community is dismissed: Ite, missa est

So he led forth his people with joy (Ps. 105: 43)

Ite, missa est—The conclusion of the mass sees the congregation dismissed with a short versicle and response:

> V The mass is ended.
> R Thanks be to God.[70]

As a versicle and response it does not invite elaborate musical
treatment. However, in the late middle ages, with the advent of
a polyphonic Ordinary in the fourteenth century, motet settings of the chant appear. Their vernacular texts and secular imagery suggest a moment of transition back to "the world"—the
introit in reverse—but the use of the motet in this liturgical position is short-lived.

Although the eucharistic action is contained within the
mass, veneration of the sacrament in the service of Benediction provides a devotional extension. Often appended to the
evening office, Benediction features the adoration of the consecrated Host with incense and eucharistic hymns ("O salu-
taris" and "Tantum ergo"). A solemn, silent blessing of the
people with the Host (often enshrined in a monstrance) marks
the service's end.

---

70. Masses omitting the Gloria, i.e. those of penitential
Advent and Lent, replace "Ite missa est" with
"Benedicamus Domino."

5

LITURGICAL MUSIC AS HOMILY

IN much of the preceding discussion we have been concerned with liturgy less as "product" than as "process," liturgy as "the doing" rather than "the done." And in several cases we have been able to establish close links between the particularities of a musical style and the furthering of a liturgical process; the plainsong gradual and the process of rhapsody or the recitative psalm tone and the process of contemplative rumination are especially vivid examples. In many cases "the doing" became done by others, acting on one's behalf. In part this reflects the diverse orders within the liturgy, each with a distinctive role to play. As in St. Paul's homily on the unity and diversity of the church, the liturgy mirrors the idea that "If the whole body were an eye, where would be the hearing? If the whole body were an ear, where would be the sense of smell?" (1 Cor: 12: 17). In part this reflects the aestheticization of the liturgy, requiring highly specialized skills for its rendition. And, closely related to this, it reflects the liturgy's growth as an arena for patronage. However, it is critical to underscore that even the richest "concert" liturgy, which, from the standpoint of patronage presumes the patron as listener, does not *ritually* presume an external audience. The liturgical music in such a context may inspire and delight, but within the liturgy it has an objective status independent of a listener. The Office psalms, for example, may be rich in aesthetic content for the pious entertainment of a patron, but that is a secondary concern from the standpoint of ritual. Ritually they are sung "because they are to be sung."

The presumption of a listener is obviously not foreign to certain aspects of the liturgy. The didactic portions of the synaxis are good examples: lessons are read *that they might be heard;* sermons are preached to *listeners.* Lessons and sermons, however, are not part of the "musical" fabric of the liturgy. Is there liturgical music directed to a listener? In certain Reformation traditions, the offering of anthem (Anglican) and cantata (Lutheran) are directed towards a listener in much the same way as the sermon. They are, in the larger sense, offered to the glory of God, but in their essence they presuppose hearers.[1] Moreover, the music, like the sermon, appears to be homiletic.

It is little surprise then that both anthem and cantata—works addressing an audience—should experience creative swells in the Baroque era, especially in the works of Henry Purcell and J. S. Bach. Significantly, the aesthetic theory of baroque music focussed on an objective musical language of the affections, directly aimed at audience response. Through a web of musical figures, keys, and scorings, each rich in affective associations, the baroque composer sought to move and arouse the listeners' passions. The music was, in essence, neither autobiographical in the Romantic sense nor functional in the medieval sense; rather, its essence was as an agency for affective response.[2] Thus, from the standpoint of musical language, the Baroque church cantata and anthem were well set

1. Though perhaps in different degrees. The anthem's descent from liturgical votive antiphons may suggest that, in theory, the anthem is more independent of audience than the cantata.

2. Cf. the distinctive paradigms of music in different historical periods outlined by Carl Dahlhaus in *Foundations of Music History,* trans. J.B. Robinson (1967; Eng. trans., Cambridge: Cambridge University Press, 1983), 20-23.

up to address listeners homiletically and, as we will see below, contemporary interest in homiletics was keen.

The Lutheran interest in preaching and the prominence it holds in the Lutheran liturgy is deeply rooted in Luther's concept of Gospel as verbal proclamation. Luther writes:

> [T]he word "Gospel" signifies nothing else than a sermon or report concerning the grace and mercy of God merited and acquired through the Lord Jesus Christ with His death. Actually, the Gospel is not what one finds in books and what is written in letters of the alphabet; it is rather an oral sermon and a living Word, a voice that resounds throughout the world and is proclaimed publically, so that one hears it everywhere.[3]

This heightened sense of Gospel as spoken proclamation is underscored by his contrasting reference to the synagogue as a "book house" and the early church as a "mouth house."[4] Preaching was a major outlet for this proclamation (though as we will see below, the cantata participates to the same end). Moreover, preaching and the eucharist—the "visible Word"[5]— were closely intertwined: preaching was to be followed by communion, communion to be preceded by preaching. In this light, the linkage between cantata texts and eucharistic imagery is significant.

Given its fundamental importance, the Lutheran sermon was preached at length and frequently. Documents from the

---

3. "Sermons on the First Epistle of St. Peter" in *Luther's Works*, ed. Jaroslav Pelikan (St. Louis: Concordia, 1967), 30: 3.

4. See Krister Stendahl, "The Word of God and the Words of Luther," in *Luther and Learning: The Wittenberg University Luther Symposium* (Selinsgrove, Pa.: Susquehanna University Press, 1985), 135.

5. Stendahl, "The Word of God," 135.

early eighteenth century in Leipzig confirm that the Sunday sermon was an hour long and that during the week they could also achieve that length. The Leipzig liturgical rota, on the evidence of Christoph Ernst Sicul (1717), provided for 22 sermons weekly.[6] If Sundays are "the Lord's"—one day in seven—we see here that approximately 22 hours of sermons alone came close to claiming the proportion of one day in the week.

Sermons in Restoration England were also prominent, though perhaps they lacked the theological underpinnings of preaching *per se* that Luther provided his followers. In the cosmopolitan world of London, the sermon was much a part of a multifaceted public life, and the reception of the sermon showed strong traces of a consumerist attitude that clouds its religious intent. Diarist Samuel Pepys on several occasions notes his practice of "church-hopping," as on March 16, 1662:

> This morning, till Churches were done, I spent going from one church to another, and hearing a bit here and a bit there.[7]

This smorgasbord approach is attitudinely significant in its implication of the need for the preacher to perform—or else! The

6. See Günther Stiller, *Johann Sebastian Bach and Liturgical Life in Leipzig*, trans. Herbert J.A. Bouman, Daniel F. Pocllot, Hilton C. Oswald, ed. Robin A. Leaver (1970; Eng. trans. St. Louis: Concordia, 1984), 53. Stiller further points out that the practice sermons of Leipzig theology students would increase the already large number of weekly sermons.

7. *The Diary of Samuel Pepys*, ed. Robert Latham and William Matthews, vol. 3 (Berkeley: Univ. of California Press, 1970), 47. For other references to sermons and diarists, see Caroline Francis Richardson, *English Preachers and Preaching* (New York: Macmillan, 1928).

criticism of sermons in seventeenth-century England was so prevalent that it suggests that one reason one might attend a sermon was indeed to criticize it. Earlier in the century the poet and preacher of St. Paul's, John Donne, admonishes:

> Because God cals Preaching *foolishnesse*, you take God at his word, and you thinke Preaching a thing under you. Hence is it, that you take so much liberty in censuring and comparing Preacher and Preacher, nay Sermon and Sermon from the same Preacher; as though we preached for wagers, and as though coine wer to be valued from the inscription meerely, and the image and the person, and not for the metall.[8]

After the Restoration, Joseph Glanvill, chaplain in ordinary to Charles II, would satirically remark to the same end:

> And indeed things had come to pass in Jerusalem that there was scarce any other use made of Preaching, but to pass judgements on the Preacher and the Sermon; which was not only undertaken by People of Age and Experience, or by those of better and advanced knowledge, but every Age was thought fit to judge here...every Rustick and Mechanick would pass absolute and definitive sentence in this matter.[9]

Pepys, as noted above, would "church hop," presumably a mode of criticism in itself. At other times his criticism took the form of slumber in the pew! Criticism might come from the organ gallery as well. John Bumpus records of the troublesome Michael Wise that

---

8. *Donne's Sermons: Selected Passages with an Essay by Logan Pearsall Smith* (Oxford: Clarendon, 1919), 18.

9. *Essays on Several Subjects in Philosophy and Religion* (1676), quoted in Richardson, *English Preachers*, 49.

being favoured by Charles II, one of his privileges was
that of playing on the organ of any church the King at-
tended. It appears that on one occasion, thinking the
sermon, probably, somewhat long and dry, he struck up
a voluntary in the middle of it, which greatly displeased
his Majesty.[10]

However, great and learned orators did indeed preach to religious and moral ends before large crowds. And the change to a
simpler style of oratory in the latter part of the century would
seem to bring the didactic intent of the sermon into sharper focus. Yet there is a lingering impression that much was calculated to impress, and, from both sides of the pulpit, performance
values were high.

A look at both anthem and cantata reveals a strong homili-
etic orientation, with some interesting interplay between the
ways of preachers and the ways of musicians. It is to these
issues that we now turn.

Restoration Anthem

The 1662 *Book of Common Prayer* allows for an anthem after
the third collect at both morning and evening prayer in "Quires
and Places where they sing." The Restoration anthem, at its
height represented by the works of Henry Purcell and John
Blow, appears in basically two forms: the "full anthem" and the
"verse anthem." The full anthem is "fully" choral and unac-
companied, a continuation of Renaissance motet ideals. The
verse anthem, on the other hand, interposes brief choral sections with more developed solo sections—the "verses"—whose
accompaniments range from basso continuo alone to instrumental ensembles providing sinfonias and ritornelli. The verse
anthem form itself was not innovative; William Byrd's famous
"Christ rising" is an important early example of the form whose

---

10. John Bumpus, *A History of English Cathedral Music*
(London: T. Werner Laurie, [n.d.])1: 142.

alternate accompaniments—organ or viol consort—show a
breadth of use in both chapel and domestic contexts. However,
the Restoration verse anthem, in the particularities of its style
is fashionably *au courant* and modishly continental. This reflects in large degree the influence of the restored monarch,
Charles II, whose French exile nurtured his taste for "fashion."
Thomas Tudway, a chorister at the Restoration, in an oft-cited
recollection explains how satisfying the royal taste—bringing
England musically up-to-date after the hiatus of the Common-
wealth—fell to young members of the Chapel Royal. Thus:

> The Standard of Church Music begun by Mr. Tal-
> lis & Mr. Bird, etc was continued for some years after
> the Restauration, and all Composers conform'd them-
> selves to the Pattern which was set by them. His Majes-
> ty who was a brisk and airy Prince, coming to the
> Crown in the flower and vigour of his age, was soon, if
> I may so say, tired with the grave and solemn way, and
> order'd the composers of his chapel to add symphonies,
> etc. with instruments to their anthems...
>
> The old masters of music...hardly knew how to
> comport themselves with these new fangl'd ways, but
> proceeded in their Compostions according to the old
> style...In about 4 or 5 years time some of the forward-
> est and brightest Children of the Chappell, as Mr.
> Humphreys, Mr. Blow, etc. began to be masters of a
> faculty of composing. This his Majesty greatly encour-
> aged by indulging their youthful fancys...In a few years
> more several others, educated in the chapel, produced
> their compositions in this style; for otherwise it was in
> vain hope to please his Majesty.[11]

The anthem then was a major arena for the introduction of
continental style (note, for example, the strong declamatory

---

11. Quoted by Charles Burney, *A General History of Music*
(London, 1789; New York: Dover, 1959) 2: 348-49.

cast of Pelham Humfrey's anthems); it was a genre close to the Stuart monarchy; and it was composed by the leading musicians of the day, in their youth and in their maturity. To appreciate its resonance with the contemporary English sermon, we must consider the sermon in closer detail.

Much of the seventeenth century in England saw a highly learned style of preaching, rich in verbal wit, thick with quotation and allusion (Greek and Latin were common), calculated to impress, atomistic in its approach to the text, exhaustingly thorough,[12] and born of a rhetorical education. This last trait is a major theme of W. Fraser Mitchell's study, *English Pulpit Oratory from Andrewes to Tillotson*. He explains:

> [I]t is plain that the English sermon in the seventeenth century bears a direct relation to the rhetorical bias of contemporary English education, in so far as the majority of those who became the preachers of the period had received the conventional training in theme, declamation, and oration. This relation must have been definitely emphasised by the practice of note-taking of vernacular sermons enjoined by the leading schoolmasters, and the close connection of the practice with the Latin exercise, so that to most seventeenth-century boys the sermon and the school exercise must have seemed inextricably combined. The young preacher setting out in life, moreover, without any practice in English composition, is bound to have regarded his first

---

12. Cf. Richardson, *English Preachers*, 36: "The thoroughness with which a text was expounded was appalling. Only a man who loved talking for its own sake would deliberately deliver one-hundred and forty-five sermons on a single chapter, as Anthony Burgess did when he gradually presented the seventeenth chapter of the Gospel of John...."

sermons as set themes on slightly different topics, to be treated in the customary way.[13]

One of the principal devices in use in such a rhetorical education was the so-called "common-place book," an anthology of quotations ready at hand for fleshing out the skeleton of a theme or oration. The process and priorities are clear in a description by Charles Hoole from 1660 on preparing a theme. As a first step, Hoole sends the student to read and then to record usable material in the common-place book. He then advises:

> let them all read what they have written before the Master and every one transcribe what others have collected into his own book; and thus they may always have store of matter for invention always at hand, which is far beyond what their own wit is able to conceive. Now to furnish themselves also with copy of good words and phrases, besides what they have collected weekly, and what hath been already said of varying them; they should have these and the like books reserved in the school Library, viz; *Sylva Synonymorum*, *Calliepeia*, Huisse's *Phrases*, *Winchester's Phrases*, Lloyd's *Phrases*, Farnaby's *Phrases* …[etc.]; and if at any time they can wittily and pithily invent anything of their own brain; you may help them to express it in good Latin, by increasing use of Cooper's *Dictionary*…[14]

It is easy to imagine then how the "quotation" sermon in its thick stew of quotation, allusion, and figure of speech is fed by

---

13. W. Fraser Mitchell, *English Pulpit Oratory from Andrewes to Tillotson* (London: SPCK, 1932), pp. 90-91.

14. Cited in Foster Watson, *The English Grammar Schools to 1660: their Curriculum and Practice* (Cambridge: Cambridge University Press, 1908), 457-458.

anthologies, published or self-compiled. And, from the evidence of the sermons, it appears the meal was an ample one.

Typical of this learned style as well is an analysis of the subject text, verse by verse or phrase by phrase, atomistically turning the words over in many different ways. The following excerpt is from an Easter Sermon preached before James I in 1620 by Lancelot Andrewes, Bishop of Winchester. His text is John 20: 11-17, the episode of Mary Magdalene in the garden on Easter morning. In the excerpt here, devoted to one of the seven verses, note not only the frequency of quotation, but also the approach to the text in fragments, the analysis and subdivision of the verse ("there are four points in it," each engendering its own discussion), and seemingly, the "wringing" as much from the text as possible.

> Ver. 16. "And saw two Angels in white, sitting, the one at the head, the other at the feet, where the body of Jesus had lain."
>
> For what came of this? Thus staying by it [the tomb], and thus looking in, again and again, though she saw not Christ at first, she sees His Angels. For so it pleased Christ to come by degrees, His Angels before Him. And it is no vulgar honour this, to see but an Angel; what would one of us give to see but the like sight?
>
> We are now at the Angels' part, their appearing in this verse. There are four points in it: 1. Their place; 2. Their habit; 3. Their site; 4. and their order. 1. Place, in the grave; 2. Habit, in white; 3. site—they were sitting; 4. and their order in sitting, one at the head, the other at the feet.
>
> 1. The place. In the grave she saw them; and Angels in a grave, is a strange sight, a sight never seen before; not till Christ's body had been there, never till this day; this the first news of Angels in that place. For a grave is no place for Angels, one would think; for worms rather: blessed Angels, not but in a blessed

place. But since Christ lay there, that place is blessed. There was a voice heard from Heaven, "Blessed be the dead:" "Precious the death," "Glorious the memory" now, "of them that die in the Lord" [Rev. 14: 13; Ps 116: 15]. And even this, that the Angels disdained not now to come thither, and to sit there, is an *auspicium* of a great change to issue in the state of that place. *Quid gloriosius Angelo? quid vilius vermiculo?* saith Augustine. *Qui fuit vermiculorum locus, est et Angelorum.* "That which was the place for worms, is become a place for Angels."

2. Their habit. "In white." So were there divers of them, divers times this day, seen, "in white" all; in that colour. It seems to be their Easter-day colour, for at this feast they all do their service in it. Their Easter-day colour, for it is the colour of the Resurrection. The state whereof when Christ would represent upon the Mount, "His raiment was all white, no fuller in the earth could come near it." [Mark 9: 3] And our colour it shall be, when rising again we "shall walk in white robes," and "follow the Lamb whithersoever He goeth." [Rev. 3: 4; Rev. 7:9; Rev. 14:4].

Heaven mourned on Good-Friday, the eclipse made all then in black. Easter-day it rejoiceth, Heaven and Angels, all in white. Solomon tells us, it is the colour of joy And that is the state of joy, and this the day of the first joyful tidings of it, with joy ever celebrated, even *in albis*, eight days together, by them that found Christ.

3. "In white," and "sitting." As the colour of joy, so the situation of rest. So we say, Sit down, and rest. And so is the grave made, by this morning's work, a place of rest. Rest, not from our labours only—so do the beasts rest when they die; but as it is in the sixteeth Psalm, a Psalm of the Resurrection, a "rest in hope"—"hope" of rising again, the members in the virtue of their Head

Who this day is risen. So to enter into the "rest," which yet "remaineth for the people of God," [Heb. 4: 9] even the Sabbath eternal.

4. "Sitting," and in this order "sitting"; "at the head one, at the feet another, where His body had lain."

(i) Which order may well refer to Christ Himself, Whose body was the true ark indeed, "in which it pleased the Godhead to dwell bodily"; [Col. 2:9] and is therefore here between two Angels, as was the ark, the type of it, "between the two cherubims." [Ex. 25: 22]

(ii) May also refer to Mary Magdalene. She had anointed His head, she had anointed His feet: at these two places sit the two Angels, as it were to acknowledge so much for her sake.

(iii) In mystery, they refer it thus. Because *caput Christi Deus*, "the Godhead is the head of Christ" [1 Cor 11:3], and His feet which the serpent did bruise, His manhood; that either of these hath his Angel. That to Christ man no less than to Christ God, the Angels do now their service. *In principio erat Verbum*, His Godhead; there, an Angel. *Verbum caro factum*, his manhood; there, another [John 1: 1, 14]. "And let all the Angels of God worship Him" in both [Heb 1: 6]. Even in His manhood, at His cradle the head of it, a choir of Angels; at His grave, the feet of it, Angels likewise.

(iv) And lastly, for our comfort thus. That henceforth even such shall our graves be, if we be so happy as to "have our parts in the first resurrection" [Rev. 20:6], which is of the soul from sin. We shall go to our graves in white, in the comfort and colour of hope, lie between two Angels there; they guard our bodies dead, and present them alive again at the Resurrection.

(i) Yet before we leave them, to learn somewhat of the Angels; specially, of "the Angel that sat at the feet." That between them there was no striving for places. He that "sat at the feet," as well content with his place as he that "at the head." We to be so by their example. For with us, both the Angels would have been "at the head," never an one "at the feet;" with us none would be at the feet by his good will, head-Angels all.

(ii) Again, from them both. That inasmuch as the head ever stands for the beginning, and the feet for the end, that we be careful that our beginnings only be not glorious—O an angel at the head in any wise—but that we look to the feet, there be another there too. *Ne turpiter atrum desinat*, "that it end not in a black Angel" [Horace], that began in a white. And this for the Angels' appearing. [15]

This style of segmented, learned preaching would endure into the Restoration era. Another of the great diarists, John Evelyn, would liken some modern preaching to the style of Bishop Andrewes (1679, 1683), [16] and preachers of a newer, simpler style would take the Andrewes model to task. In the last part of the century, with Robert South, Isaac Barrow, and John Tillotson, preaching takes on a plainer style in tune with reforms of the Royal Society. A contemporary chronicler of the Royal Society, Thomas Sprat (1667) speaks of this reform:

They [the members of the Royal Society] have therefore been more rigorous in putting in Execution the only Remedy, that can be found for this *Extravagance* [of language], and that has been, a constant Resolution to reject all Amplifications, Digressions, and Swellings of Style; to return back to the primitive purity and

15. *Ninety-Six Sermons by the Right Honourable and Reverend Father in God, Lancelot Andrewes...* (Oxford: John Henry Parker, 1841), 8-11.

16. See *The Diary of John Evelyn*, ed. E.S. de Beer (Oxford: Clarendon Press, 1955), 4: 166 [4 April, 1679] and 4: 330 [15 July, 1683].

Shortness, when men deliver'd so many *Things* almost in an equal number of *Words*.[17]

Judging from contemporary comment, it seems that affectivity—moving the passions—was, as in music, an important issue in the sermon's rendition as well. For example, one contemporary criticism of memorized sermons, like those of the dissenters,' was that their lack of spontaneity blinded them to the affective context:

> a man cannot ordinarily be so much affected himself (and consequently he cannot so much affect others) with things he speaks by rote; as when he takes some liberty to prosecute a matter according to his own immediate apprehension appear in the Auditory.[18]

Similarly, jurist John Selden writes that:

> The tone in preaching does much in working upon the Peoples' Affections. If a Man should make Love in an ordinary Tone, his Mistress would not regard him; and therefore he must whine. If a man should cry Fire, or Murther in an Ordinary Voice, nobody would come to help him.[19]

Moreover, weeping was held to be "a legitimate elocutionary aid to impressiveness."[20]

17. *The History of the Royal Society of London* quoted by James Winn, in *John Dryden and His World* (New Haven: Yale University Press, 1987), 13, and Mitchell, p. 332.

18. Cited in Mitchell, *English Pulpit Oratory*, 21.

19. Cited in Richardson, *English Preachers*, 54.

20. Richardson, *English Preachers*, 56.

To summarize, a learned style of preaching, scholastically rhetorical and rich in quotation was well established in seventeenth-century England and persisted into the Restoration, often taking the form of analytical divisions which atomize the text in order to bring forth multiple meanings from it. Though it occasioned memorable prose from the likes of Lancelot Andrewes, one senses the danger of the manner in lesser hands, especially given its frequent reliance on common-place books. The end of the century, as noted above, sees a simpler style, shorn of quotation and direct in language.

What might a musical equivalent look like? A good example is Purcell's "They that go down to the sea in ships," an anthem colorfully described by Franklin Zimmerman as "a thanksgiving piece commemorating the miraculous salvation of Charles II, James, duke of York, and John Gostling from shipwreck during an outing on the royal yacht 'The Fubs,' so named because of its broad beam, a feature it shared with the duchess of Portsmouth, along with this sobriquet."[21] The text set is Ps. 107: 23-32.

23. They that go down to the sea in ships; …
24. These men see the works of the Lord, and his wonders in the deep.
25. For at his word the stormy wind ariseth, which lifteth up the waves thereof.
26. They are carried up to heav'n, and down again to the deep; their soul melteth away because of trouble.
27. They reel to and fro, and stagger like a drunken man, and are at their wit's end.

21. Franklin Zimmerman, *Henry Purcell 1659-1695: His Life and Times* (Philadelphia: University of Pennsylvania Press, 1983), xxx. The bass solos in the anthem, replete with their low D's, were sung by Gostling, well known for his vocal profundity. For the score, see *The Works of Henry Purcell*, ed. by Anthony Lewis and Nigel Fortune (London: Novello, 1962), 32.

28. So when they cry unto the Lord in their trouble, he delivereth them out of their distress.

29. For he maketh the storm to cease, so that the waves thereof are still.

30. Then are they glad because they are at rest; and so he bringeth them unto the hav'n where they would be.

31. O that men would therefore praise the Lord for his goodness; and declare the wonders that he doth for the children of men!

32. That they would exalt him also in the congregation of the people, and praise him in the seat of the elders!

Its form, typical of Purcell's large-scale verse anthems, juxtaposes solo and choral textures in sections delineated by instrumental ritornelli. The whole form is set in motion by a lengthy sinfonia, evocative of the French overture.

THEY THAT GO DOWN TO THE SEA IN SHIPS

SINFONIA mm. 1–37	BASS VERSE mm. 38–103	RITORNELLO mm. 104–115	ALTO-BASS VERSE mm. 116–151	RITORNELLO mm. 152–179
D maj	D maj	D maj	d min	d min
bipartite	vv. 23-27		vv. 28-29	
Fr. overture	rich in text painting			

(continued…)

ALTO-BASS VERSE mm. 180–196	RITORNELLO mm. 197–204	ALTO-BASS VERSE mm. 205–245	RITORNELLO mm. 245–256	CHORUS mm. 257–277
D maj	D maj	D maj	D maj	D maj
v. 30		vv. 31-32		v. 31 in part

In terms of its musical vocabulary, the most readily apparent feature is Purcell's commanding use of text painting. An expectation of the style, indeed, but moreover something that is particularly invited by the succession of vivid images in the psalm, ranging from stormy winds and melting souls to the wobbly legs of the ship-borne in a tempest. Purcell isolates each image in a vivid representation:

> "down to the sea in ships"
>> a two-octave descent to low D for the solo bass

> "stormy wind ariseth"
>> tempestuous dotted figures rise through the compass of an octave and a half.

> "carried up to heav'n, and down again to the deep"
>> a familiar play on contour, with "deep" underscored by (again) low D for the solo bass.

> "their soul melteth away"
>> chromatic alterations

> "and stagger like a drunken man"
>> lombard rhythms (short–long, iambic figures)

The examples are vivid and impressive, but also rhetorical stereotypes—commonplace figures of musical rhetoric, analogous to the verbal figures of speech employed by the oratorical preacher. Their presence here may well remind of the preachers' interest in wit. Joseph Glanvill, in his 1678 *An Essay Concerning Preaching* states that "Wit in the Imagination [is] a quickness in the phancy, *to give things proper Images.*"[22] And, of course, giving things their "proper image" is what Purcell is doing in this first section. The "images" are largely clustered in the opening

---

22. Cited in Mitchell, *English Pulpit Oratory,* 6. Emphasis added.

verse, owing to the nature of the text. It is a notable irony then that the closing words of the section note that "they are at their wit's end"!

Harmony also plays a part in the rhetorical enhancement of the anthem. The melodic figure of "melteth away because of trouble" seems both to ooze and suffer to greater effect for its introduction of diminished sonority. On a larger scale the modal contrast of D major and d minor effectively contrasts the "troubled" and "rescued" elements of the psalm, a typical psalmodic antithesis that here finds a translation in key.

Much then supports a view of this as "rhetorical." And again, this is an expectation of seventeenth-century English style, as the writings of Henry Peacham, the Elder, John Hoskyns, Henry Peacham, the younger, Francis Bacon, and Charles Butler suggest.[23] For it to be homiletical, we must consider the message of the music. To what ends its rhetoric? In terms of a pious message, we may look to the figurative unity of "stormy wind" and "gladdness." Both figures rely on similar rising dotted figures (cf. mm. 53-56 and 180-183), a commonality that suggests that the storm is *transformed* into the gladness. In part this is a traditional message of Christian salvation in the form of rescue from distress. However, Purcell's use of transformation additionally suggests the *unity* of the storm and the rescue, a musical illustration of the paradoxical tenet of Christian spirituality that finds in suffering its own relief.

Not surprisingly, there is something of a political message as well. The opening sinfonia's evocation of the French overture provides a musical icon of royalty. That, and the influence of Charles II on the anthem form itself, as Tudway attests, invite a monarchical reading of the anthem, whose splendor

---

23. See Gregory Butler, "Music and Rhetoric in Early Seventeenth-Century English Sources," *Musical Quarterly* 66 (1980): 53-64.

reflects brightly on the patronal power that brought it into being. The psalm text suggests that God will save the righteous. The monarchical quotation marks around the anthem fine-tunes the message: God will save and has saved *this* righteous King. Moreover, one might adduce the King's righteousness on the basis *of* the rescue from nautical mishap with the royal yacht that occasioned the anthem in the first place.

The use of the anthem politically need not surprise. In an age where monarchs ruled by divine right, the wall between church and state was permeable, especially, one presumes, in defense of that divine right and the monarch it legitimized. Psalmodic texts, as well, allegorically associate King Charles with King David, and in several instances, especially with judicious selection of verses, offer topical comment.[24] The David-Charles allegory was particularly strong in treating the issues relating to the succession of the throne and the claims of Charles' bastard son, James, Duke of Monmouth, as seen, for example, in Dryden's well-known poem "Absalom and Achitophel" (1681).[25]

If we see Purcell's anthem (and others like it) in a homiletic light, we might well wish to underscore its ties to the spoken sermon. If it is a sermon from the choir stalls, in what ways is it like the sermon from the pulpit? Several points are compelling.

1. Both are highly fashioned rhetorical arrangements with common affective goals for their perceived listeners. (The affectivity of music in general and church music in particular was treated at some length in the English Cecilian tradition. Vari-

24. See Zimmerman, *Henry Purcell*, 64-65, for allegorical readings of "I will love Thee, O Lord" and "Jehovah quam multi sunt hostes."

25. See *Dryden: Poems and Prose*, sel. Douglas Grant (Harmondsworth, Eng.: Penguin Books, 1985), 16–50.

ous odes to St. Cecilia emphasize the specificity of affective musical response, as in, for example, Dryden's "A Song for St. Cecilia's Day" (1687), whose thesis is couched in the memorable line "What passion cannot music raise and quell!")[26] The correspondences would certainly include, as noted above, the analogy between verbal wit and text painting, both seeking "to give things proper Images." And in that the musical figuration associated with text painting was often stereotypical it invites an analogy with the preachers' recourse to common-place books and phrase books.

In structure as well, the sectionalized nature of the sermon finds an echo in the strong delineation of verse sections in the anthem with changing key, scoring, style, and ritornello. Moreover, with the sermon's divisions, the analytical fragmentation of the text is not unlike the madrigalistic isolation of individual words in the musical unfolding of the text. As the preacher stops to consider each phrase in turn, so too the composer.

---

26. Significantly, surviving sermons preached on St. Cecilia's Day use music's affectivity in defense of elaborate music in church. Charles Hickman, for instance, in his Cecilia Sermon from 1695 observes that worship is "the workings of an exalted Love; the outgoings of an inflam'd Desire; the breathings of a pious Soul, in the extasies of his Joy and Admiration." And further, that music was to "adorn their [all lands'] Religious Worship, and inspire them with pious, exalted, devout Affections; not to gratify their itching Ears; but to refine their Notions, abstract their Thoughts, and prepare their Souls for Heavenly Contemplations." See Charles H. Bikle, "A Brief Analysis of Three Sermons Preached on St. Cecilia's Day in London During the 1690's" in *Music from the Middle Ages through the Twentieth Century: Essays in Honor of Gwynn S. McPeek*, ed., Carmelo P. Comberiati and Matthew C. Steel (New York: Gordon and Breach, 1988), 183.

2. It is difficult to mistake Purcell's relish of rich imagery and delight in descriptive detail. This seems to suggest at least a spiritual kinship with the old-fashioned preaching style of Jeremy Taylor, Bishop of Down and Connor following the Restoration. John Chandos writes of Taylor that it

> sometimes seems as if, intoxicated by the prodigality of his imagination, he is about to drown in his own words. But just as he is on the point of plunging under one foaming simile too many, never to surface more, he reappears, swimming, dolphin-like, with lyrical ease…[27]

For example, in a 1653 sermon on gluttony, Taylor, to mutual delight I suspect, goes "the long way around" to make a simple point vivid, descriptive, and even alluring:

> When *Cyrus* had espyed *Astynages* and his fellowes coming drunk from a banquet, loaden with variety of follies and filthinesse, their legs failing them, their eyes red and staring, cousened with a moist cloud, and abused by a doubled object, their tongues full as spunges, and their heads no wiser, he thought they were poysoned, and he had reason; for what malignant quality can be more venomous and hurtfull to a man then the effect of an intemperate goblet, and a full stomach?…
>
> He that tempts me to drink beyond my measure, civilly invites me to a feaver; and to lay aside my reason, as the *Persian* women did their garments and their modesty at the end of feasts ….[28]

The wealth of detail and image seems close indeed to the pic-

---

27. John Chandos, *In God's Name* (Indianapolis: Bobbs-Merrill, 1971), 482.

28. Chandos, *In God's Name*, 500-01.

torial catalog we find in the opening verse of Purcell's anthem.

3. With Taylor close at hand, it is fruitful to propose one further analogy, viz, the free admixture of the sacred and the profane. The pedigree of Purcell's anthem draws on a madrigal aesthetic for its treatment of the text and a French theatre style for its overture and the gaiety of its triple-meter dance sections. Similarly, Taylor is known for intermingling images. One observer cites, for example, the following passage that proposes that the hope of eternal life will

> make a satyr chast, and Silenus to be sober, and Dives to be charitable, and Simon Magus to despise reputation, and Saul to turn from a Persecutor to an Apostle.[29]

As the preacher ranged widely and freely in choice of image, so too the composer in choice of idiom.

Lutheran Cantata

The Lutheran church cantata takes several forms in its heyday during the Baroque era, ranging from conservative settings of chorale poetry or scripture to settings of "libretti" that introduce the modern poet's hand in textually diverse works combining scripture, chorale, chorale and scriptural paraphrase, and "free" poetry. With this latter style of cantata, prominently associated with poets like the Weissenfels cleric Erdmann Neumeister, the cantata takes on the trappings of the operatic scene: active recitative—contemplative da capo aria. And while conservative voices would decry this theatricality, Neumeister was clear in his intention and vigorous in his defense:

> To express myself shortly, a *cantata* seems to be nothing else than a portion of an opera composed of *stylo recitativo* and arie together.[30]

---

29. Mitchell, *English Pulpit Oratory*, 248.

This unambiguous view appeared in the preface to his first collection of cantata libretti (1704). And in that same preface he seeks to deflect criticism by citing other secularisms that seemed to be capable of sanctification.

> I will not strive to justify myself in this matter till first I am answered: Why certain other spiritual songs are not done away with which are of the same *genus versuum* as worldly, nay often profane songs? Why the *instrumenta musica* are not broken which we hear in churches today and which only yesterday were performed upon for the luxury of worldly pleasure? And hence, whether this kind of poetry, though it has borrowed its model from theatrical verse, may not be sanctified by being dedicated to the service of God.[31]

The cantata's rooting in the *de tempore* scripture readings (*pericopes*) and chorales tie it closely to the liturgy of the day. Its potential to interpret, inflect, and comment upon the *pericopes* was strong, especially in cantatas with modern texts. Many have asserted the view that the cantata—particularly J. S. Bach's—should be viewed as musical sermons.[32] The idea of a "musical sermon" is associated with the views of Luther, as Günther Stiller underscores. He observes that

30. In Philip Spitta, *Johann Sebastian Bach* (1889; Eng. trans., New York: Dover, 1951)   1: 473.

31. Spitta, *Bach* 1: 478-79.

32. See for example Friedrich Blume's adulatory view in *Protestant Church Music: A History* (New York, 1974), 282 or Stiller, *Bach and Liturgical Life*, 167, 213, and 221. See also Robin A. Leaver, "The Liturgical Place and Homiletic Purpose of Bach's Cantatas," *Worship* 59 (1985): 194–202; and Robin A. Leaver, *J.S. Bach as Preacher: His Passions and Music in Worship* (St. Louis: Concordia, 1982).

> Luther already wanted to see music employed exclu-
> sively "in the service of exegesis and of the enlivening of
> the Word," that he had in mind "a musical exegesis that
> might intensify the Biblical text through melodic,
> rhythmic, harmonic, and contrapuntal means and
> might thus let it strike the hearer in full force," indeed
> that Luther himself...used the expression *klingende*
> *Predigt* (musical sermon).[33]

Contemporary evidence was close at hand as well. Neumeister,
again in reference to his 1704 collection of librettos speaks of
them as growing out of his sermons:

> When arranging the regular services of the Sunday I en-
> deavoured to render the most important subjects treat-
> ed of in my sermon in a compact and connected form
> for my own private devotions, and so to refresh myself
> after the fatigue of preaching by such pleasing exercises
> of the mind. Whence arose now an ode, now a poetical
> oration, and with them the present cantatas.[34]

Furthermore, Bach's copy of *Calov's Bible Commentary* is rich in
its implications. Surviving with the composer's underlining and
marginalia, it offers a rare window through which we glimpse
something of the piety behind the notes. In Calov's preface to
the Psalter, Bach has marked for emphasis a text which associates the office of prophecy with music.[35] Although only an oblique reference to the notion of cantata as sermon, its
association with the master of the genre heightens its significance.

---

33. Stiller, *Bach and Liturgical Life*, 150.

34. Spitta, *Bach*, 1: 473.

35. See Robin A. Leaver, ed., *J.S. Bach and Scripture: Glosses
from the Calov Bible Commentary* (St. Louis: Concordia,
1985), 30, 99-101.

The position of the cantata within the liturgy emphasized its didactic function as well, and nurtured a close relationship to the sermon. The cantata was sung after the Gospel (upon which it would be based) and before the singing of the Creed. In Leipzig documents, we find the Creed followed by the "pulpit service" of which the re-reading of the Gospel and the sermon was the centerpiece. If the cantata were structurally in two parts, the second part would come at the end of the pulpit service, thus providing a musical frame for the sermon on a closely related theme, as was the case with two-part Passions.[36] A contemporary account of the Leipzig memorial service for Queen Christiane Eberhardine in 1727 suggests that this framing idea was active in other liturgical contexts as well:

> When, then, everyone had taken his place, there had been an improvisation on the organ, and the ode of Mourning... had been distributed among those present by the Beadles, there was shortly heard the Music of Mourning which this time Capellmeister Johann Sebastian Bach had composed in Italian style..., half being

36. Stiller, *Bach and Liturgical Life*, 124. Stiller speculates that perhaps more cantatas were performed split around the sermon than those designated as two-part works (p. 80). He also interestingly suggests the possible use of the second part of the cantata as communion music, a view supported by the eucharistic nature of some cantata texts (p. 82). Whether sung during communion or not, the presence of eucharistic texts in the cantata gives weight both to the integrality of the liturgy and Luther's own close linkage of the sermon and the communion.

The editors of the *Bach Reader* as well suggest that in Bach's manuscript "Order of Divine Service in Leipzig" found in the manuscript for BWV 61, the "composition" following the Words of Institution of the Sacrament is likely the second part of the cantata. See p. 70.

heard before and half after the oration of praise and mourning.[37]

The musical frame for the sermon is not unique to the Lutheran liturgy; the two-part oratorio in seventeenth-century Italy was performed in the same fashion, insuring a "captive" audience for the sermon in the evangelistic meetings of the oratory.

One might imagine that in a three- to four- hour liturgy, of which one hour was the sermon, the cantata afforded some measure of pious diversion. However, the didactic intent extended to providing copies of the text for the congregation, and, presumably to stress graphically its foundations, scriptural passages were highlighted. Some used the time in collateral devotions (in spirit, not unlike the use of the rosary at mass) though this was open to criticism.[38] Clearly, this was not a time for "passive" listening.

The sophistication and theatricality of the modern cantata found it a place in Orthodox Lutheran churches and kept it distant from Pietistic ones. Orthodox and Pietist sectarianism reflected a pronounced tension within the church between, on the one hand, a high degree of formalism and emphasis on the learned consideration of dogma, and, on the other, a more individual and explicitly emotional approach to worship. This latter approach, the Piestist way associated with Jakob Spener whose *Pia Desideria* (1675) was a foundational expression of the movement's ideals, grew in reaction to perceived excesses of formalism. Scholar Gerald Cragg typically characterizes the church in the wake of the Thirty Years War as one in which

37. See *The Bach Reader*, ed. Hans David and Arthur Mendel (New York: W.W. Norton, 1966), 113.

38. Stiller, *Bach and Liturgical Life*, 121, 122, 216, 265.

The intellect was in the ascendant, and in a particularly arid form, while vast and intricate dogmatic systems fortified the rival positions of Lutheran and Calvinist theologians. There was no perception of the symbolical character of much religious thought. Disputation had become the accepted method by which religious truth was enforced, indeed the prevailing spirit which governed church life. Strict orthodoxy became an obsession. Logic, pedantry, and the parade of learning had sometimes usurped the central place even in worship...[A]t times the sermon provided a pretext for the parade of abstruse and irrelevant knowledge.[39]

Again, the "parade" did not sweep up all in its motion; Spener and his followers travelled a more subjectively inclined path. The Pietists eschewed elaborate music like the cantata in favor of simple, strophic hymns. In the Orthodox context, however, it is easy to hear in the cantata a voice of subjective piety in both text and music. In some circumstances it may have provided an emotional balance to a cerebral liturgy of the pulpit. But it is dangerous to limit the reality of the situation to unmediated extremes.[40] Jaroslav Pelikan interjects the appropriate degree of caution:

> [I]t is probably accurate to guess that most of Bach's theological and clerical contemporaries would not be classified as either consistent Pietists or thorough Rationalists or unambiguously Orthodox...[41]

39. Gerald Cragg, *The Church and the Age of Reason* (Harmondsworth, Eng.: Penguin Books, 1960), 99-100.

40. Cf. Stiller, *Bach and Liturgical Life*, 99 on the mystical element in Orthodoxy.

41. *Bach Among the Theologians* (Philadelphia: Fortress Press, 1986), 57. See also Robin A. Leaver, "Bach and Pietism," *Concordia Theological Quarterly* 55 (1991): 5–22.

Bach's pulpit language through which he offers "living" proclamation of the Gospel and through which the redemptive action of an incarnate God is piously put forth vested in the "incarnational" tones of human affectivity is formed of several important elements. He draws on stereotypical rhetorical figures, a rich vocabulary of musical associations (contextual meanings evoked by forms, instrumentation, and pre-existent melody), and a facility at adapting musical structure to rhetorical ends.

It is unnecessary to treat Bach's use of pictorial, rhetorical figures at any length. As a German Baroque composer, he used them liberally and effectively, but this should not strike us as extraordinary. A more revealing view of his creative homiletics emerges in considering his use of associative constructions. In his cantata for Advent Sunday, 1714, "Nun komm der Heiden Heiland," BWV 61, the opening movement presents the first stanza of Luther's *de tempore* chorale, "Nun komm der Heiden Heiland," an adaptation of the medieval Latin hymn "Veni redemptor gentium." The text itself—"Saviour of the nations, come"—and the fact that it was the hymn of the day strongly rooted the cantata in the context of the seasonal liturgy. However, the Gospel for the day was the dramatic and imageful triumphal entry into Jerusalem, the entry of a King (Matthew 21: 1-9). Surprisingly, the librettist Neumeister foregoes the *pericope;* the libretto neither here nor subsequently refers to Jesus' kingship,[42] yet it is as king that the Gospel portrays him. The librettist's more general approach is brought back to Gospel particularity by Bach's skillful homiletic use of associations. In the opening movement, he innovatively writes a chorale fantasia in the unmistakable form of the French overture, a rare if not unique example. In so doing, because of the royal

---

42. Excepting perhaps the oblique reference to *Freudenkrone* (crown of joy) in the final chorale fragment.

imagery fully associated with the French overture, Luther's chorale melody and text are wed to the Gospel *pericope* in a creative and convincing union.

The genesis of the French overture within the court of Louis XIV, a court of unrivalled monarchical *ambience*, gave Bach's use of the form clarity of meaning, a meaning that was part of the social fabric of the day. Other associations were derived from within the community itself. The chorale repertory, for example, offered readily identifiable *musical* icons of *textual* ideas explicit in their poetry. Thus, for instance, in another cantata with Advent associations "Wachet, betet," BWV 70, the bass recitative "Ach soll nicht dieser grosser Tag" presents a horrific eschatological vision with trembling bass, angular contours, and violent string cascades, all ushered in by an unusual initial diminished sonority (Example 14 on page 157). At measure 5 the text speaks of the "solemn trumpet call"—the Last Trumpet of 1 Cor. 15. At this point, Bach logically introduces the trumpet in the orchestra, but with the fine touch that it plays the chorale melody "Es ist gewisslich an der Zeit," a German metrical version of the Dies Irae, the foreboding medieval sequence for a Requiem. In quoting this melody, Bach opens a window on all that its text connotes, and in so doing, adds a measure of additional gravity to his scene of the world in collapse. He further uses the harmonic expectations of the chorale—here unfulfilled—to arouse the hearer's fear. The straightforward melody implies straightforward harmony. Bach, however, plays against these expectations to strong effect (Example 15 on page 159). In a sense, this nightmarish harmony of the chorale interprets the associative meanings of its silent text.

The associative references used by Bach obviously rely on externals for their meaning. In other cases his constructions are self-referential, deriving their meaning from within the work itself. Staying with the Advent cantatas, Cantata 61 again offers a good example. The third movement is a tenor da capo aria in ritornello form. The text beckons:

> Come, Jesus, come to your church,
> and give a blessed new year!

Example 14. J.S. Bach, *Wachet, betet*, BWV 70/9 (mm. 1–6)

The emphasis on the invitational verb "come" underscores a central Advent theme, although there is little in the text to inflect it, that is, to personalize it or steer it affectively. Bach's ritornello, however, is of interest in this regard. For much of its course the ritornello (Example 16 on page 159) follows an even and predictable path. Melodically, the C-major cadence is prepared in the outline of the dominant-seventh sonority on the downbeats of mm. 11-13 (enclosed). And in m. 14 the melodic set-up for resolution is strong. Strikingly unexpected then is the octave leap to the leading tone in measure 15 and the cadence delay which follows. This heightening of the leading tone underscores a sense of *expectancy*—in the music and in Advent. As the leading tone embodies the expectation of resolution, the listener transfers this dynamic to the text, now inflected by musical means.

Example 15. J. S. Bach, *Es ist gewisslich an der Zeit*

(a) traditional expectations

(b) BWV 70 (reduction)

Example 16. J.S. Bach, *Nun Komm der Heiden Heiland,* BWV 61/3 (mm. 1–17)

Example 17. J.S. Bach, *Aus der Tiefe*, BWV 131

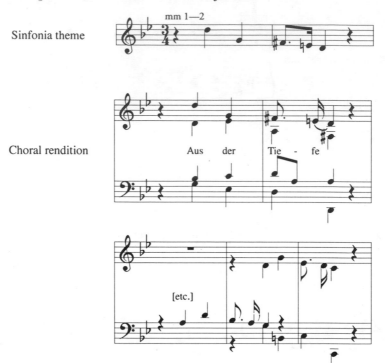

A more large-scale example of similar thinking may be found in Bach's early cantata, "Aus der Tiefe," BWV 131 (1707), a setting of Ps. 130. The theme of the psalm and Bach's sermon upon it is encapsulated in the opening and concluding verses:

> Out of the depths do I cry to thee O Lord! Lord hear my voice! Let thy ears be attentive to the voice of my supplication. O Israel, hope in the Lord, for with the Lord there is steadfast love and with him is plenteous redemption. And he will redeem Israel from all the iniquities of Israel.

The sins of Israel prompt the cry "out of the depths," but Israel will be heard and redeemed by the Lord. The antithesis of the verses engenders Bach's musical game: in *musical terms*, a struggle to ascend, to overcome the depths. These depths are well established in the opening sinfonia and chorus both by motivic contour and staggering bass range (Example 17 on page 160). That this prevailing descent is to be countered—sin is to be struggled against—is given brief glimpses in rising cross relations or, more strikingly in the passage shown below in Example 18. Here successive vocal entries are stacked up to create a rising tetrachord in suspension. And that this ascent is not easily achieved is suggested by the accompanying chromatic rise in the bass. These are again but brief suggestions that the depths are to be countered. Appropriately, the strongest answer to descent is found in the hopeful last movement. Its spirited fugue presents the following subject and countersubject (Example 19 on page 162):

Example 18. J.S. Bach, *Aus der Tiefe*, BWV 131 (mm. 39–43)

This division of the text between subject and countersubject is significant as is the nature of the melodies themselves.

1. Both melodies are strong figures of ascent: a three-fold rising sequence in the subject and rising chromatic fourth in the countersubject.

2. The extreme melismatic nature of the subject strongly suggests a freedom in redemption (*erlösen*); the chromatic rise through the interval of a fourth depicts not only the struggle to ascend—i.e. bit by bit—but also stereotypically associates the struggle with sin, a reading confirmed by its text: *aus allen seinen Sünden*.

3. The importance of the rise through the fourth is strongly presaged earlier in the movement in association with "redemption" (Example 20 on page 163), and may also be heard as a victorious inversion of the opening "der Tiefe" (Example 21 on page 163).

Example 19. J.S. Bach, *Aus der Tiefe*, BWV 131 (mm. 313–317)

Example 20. J.S. Bach, *Aus der Tiefe*, BWV 131 (mm. 307–310)

Thus, in strictly musical terms, cantata 131 seeks a balance between descent and ascent, and in so doing metaphorically enacts the struggle inherent in the text. And while the opening line of the psalm inspires the game (depths/descent), the musical response is not pictorial—there are no words of "ascent" to be painted in the music—but rather structural. And Bach's use of musical structure to such ends is an important part of his creative response to the homiletical challenge of his office.

Example 21. J.S. Bach, *Aus der Tiefe*, BWV 131

6

CODA

"*Possibly sound—like the gods a powerful unseen presence—is an unacknowledged model for our concept of the other worldly.*"[1]

IN Bartolomeo Montagna's *Madonna and Child* (1494), Mary sits enthroned as *Regina coeli*, Queen of Heaven. At her feet are two lutenists; one tunes his instrument, its courses brought into harmony, and thereby the two players are also brought into harmony, one with the other.[2] Their presence and their activity here brings Mary's role as mediatrix into view: through her agency—her intercession, but especially her role as *Theotokos*, bearer of God, the redeemer—things are *brought into accord*. Within the complementary resonance of the lute strings lies a metaphorical richness, hinted at from time to time in the preceding pages, and one that might briefly sound the final notes of this essay. We have seen ways in which music as a process, as a verb, has furthered liturgical ends, and how the specifics of a

1. David Burrows, *Sound, Speech, and Music* (Amherst: University of Massachusetts Press, 1990), 25.

2. For similar depictions, see Bernardino di Mariotto's *Madonna and Child in Glory,* (1512-14) and the *Madonna and Child Enthroned* by Defendente Ferrari (c. 1520), Girolamo Di Benvenuto (1508), and Cosimo Tura (c. 1474).

given style may be illumined with the light of its devotional intention. And we have seen ways in which music as an object, as
a noun, has played a strong role in addressing listeners homilec-
tically. In both cases, it has been music in its particularity that
has been before us. However, the lutenists in Montagna's painting do not offer music in its "particularity;" rather, they offer
music in its generality—music as sound—as a metaphor for
God's presence in the world.

The intertwining of thinking about God and music was
strong in the Middle Ages, especially through the long-lived
writings of Boethius in which a cosmic harmony re-echoed in
human nature as well as in music that was heard. And in the
harmony could be perceived the face of God. Sound had the
potential to be theophanic because it revealed the order of creation and that order was indelibly stamped with the face of the
creator. Similarly too, the "great chain of being" stretching
"from the foot of God's throne to the meanest of inanimate
objects"[3] gave form to the idea of the interrelatedness of creation and unity in its diversity. Its chain-link imagery may find
a sonic expression in the behavior of the overtone series. The
span of the overtone series ranging from lowest fundamental
to highest partial suggests in itself the all-embracing scope of
the chain, while the interrelatedness of the links is suggested in
the containment of all the partials within the one fundamental. To sound the fundamental is to bring, in varying degrees,
all of the tones in the series alive: *Deus creator* at the extreme of
one chain becomes the generating sonic fundament of the
other.

Several recent studies have highlighted the distinctiveness
of sound in the human experience.[4] And one compelling idea
that emerges is that sound is experienced *within* the hearer,

3. E.M.W. Tillyard, *The Elizabethan World Picture* (New
York: Vintage Books, [n.d.]), 26.

though conceding at the same time an objective source for the sound from *without* the hearer. We may perceive that the sound comes from "over there," but we don't hear it "over there"; our *sensation* of the sound is an internal phenomenon; We hear it as it vibrates within us physically and psychologically, regardless of where it comes from. Of the senses, touch and sight retain a strong notion of their objective source—an otherness—in the sensation itself. For me to *see* something is to see it located externally to myself; similarly, to touch presupposes that that which is touched is "other" than that which touches (one may indeed touch oneself—the fingertip may touch the leg—but the fingertip cannot touch itself any more than the eye can see itself). Smell and hearing on the other hand, perhaps owing to the incorporeality of their essence, seem to invade our inner field in the sensation. They come to us "spirit-like"[5] and travel across the gulf of subject and object, self and other.

It is this diminishing of the gap between self and other[6] that ultimately gives sound—and music—its greatest theologi-

---

4. See, for example, John Shepherd's *Music as a Social Text.* Shepherd proposes distinctions between the relatedness of sound and the objectivity of sight. See also Burrows, *Sound, Speech, and Music.* Burrows too contrasts sight and sound to strong effect: "The field of vision is a swiveling cone of receptivity, like a reverse-flow searchlight with which we scan our surroundings. But we stop to listen: inwardly, listening may be just as active as looking, but outwardly we will often arrest movement and wait for the sound to come clear. Seeing is like touching, hearing like being touched; except that the touch of sound does not stop at the skin." (p. 21).

5. Little surprise that sound and smell play such prominent roles in ritual. Clearly all the senses have spiritual capability and may be ritually employed, but the nature of sound and smell make them especially rich.

cal capacity. Like God who is in all things, thus a Divine
Other and an indwelling Spirit, sound bids us respond to an
otherness that has sought us out, but will take on life as it res-
onates within.

---

6. Cf. Burrows on making sound for oneself: "people who
hum or whistle to themselves can achieve a temporary
omniscience, since they are provisionally both self and
other; or what perhaps amounts to the same thing, they
achieve a temporary return to that stage of infantile
consciousness in which no division is made between within
and without and the world is the resonance of self." *Sound,
Speech, and Music*, 36.

FOR FURTHER READING

General

Bouyer, Louis. *Liturgical Piety.* Notre Dame: University of Notre Dame Press, 1955.

Clarke, W.K. Lowther, ed. *Liturgy and Worship.* London: SPCK, 1954.

Dix, Gregory, OSB. *The Shape of the Liturgy* [1945]. New York: Seabury Press, 1982.

Falconer, Keith. "Ritual Reflections." In *Companion to Medieval & Renaissance Music,* ed. Tess Knighton and David Fallows, 69–73. New York: Schirmer, 1992.

Harper, John. *The Forms and Orders of Western Liturgy from the Tenth to the Eighteenth Century.* Oxford: Clarendon Press, 1991.

Hiley, David. *Western Plainchant.* Oxford: Oxford University Press, 1993.

James, E. O. *Christian Myth and Ritual: A Historical Study.* Cleveland: World Publishing, 1965.

McKinnon, James. *Music and Society: Antiquity and the Middle Ages.* Englewood Cliffs, N.J.: Prentice Hall, 1990.

_____. *Music in Early Christian Literature.* Cambridge: Cambridge University Press, 1987.

The Oxford Illustrated History of Christianity, ed. John McManners. Oxford: Oxford University Press, 1990.

The Study of Liturgy, ed. Cheslyn Jones, et al. New York: Oxford University Press, 1992.

Thompson, Bard, ed. *Liturgies of the Western Church*. Philadelphia: Fortress Press, 1961.

Preface

Kleinig, John W. *The Lord's Song: The Basis, Function and Significancy of Choral Music in Chronicles*. Sheffield: Sheffield Academic Press, 1993.

Lamb, John A. *The Psalms in Christian Worship*. London: Faith Press, 1962.

Chapter 1

Berman, Morris. *Coming to Our Senses: Body and Spirit in the Hidden History of the West*. New York: Bantam Books, 1989.

Bouyer, Louis. *Liturgical Piety*. Notre Dame: University of Notre Dame Press, 1955.

Crichton, J. D. "A Theology of Worship." In *The Study of Liturgy*, 3–31. New York: Oxford University Press, 1992.

Harrison, Frank Ll. "Music and Cult: the Functions of Music in Social and Religious Systems." In *Perspectives in Musicology*, ed. Barry S. Brook, et al., 307–334. New York: Norton, 1973.

Leclercq, Jean, OSB. *The Love of Learning and the Desire for God*. New York: Fordham University Press, 1977.

Wainwright, Geoffrey. *Doxology*. Oxford: Oxford University Press, 1980.

Chapter 2

Bouyer, Louis. *Liturgical Piety.* Notre Dame: University of Notre Dame Press, 1955.

Bradshaw, Paul. *The Search for the Origins of Christian Worship.* New York: Oxford University Press, 1992.

Bynum, Caroline Walker. "Did the Twelfth Century Discover the Individual?" In *Jesus as Mother: Studies in the Spirituality of the High Middle Ages*, 82–109. Berkeley: University of California Press, 1982.

Eliade, Mircea. *Cosmos and History: The Myth of the Eternal Return.* New York: Harper Torchbooks, 1959.

_____. *The Sacred and the Profane: The Nature of Religion.* New York: Harcourt Brace Jovanovich, 1959.

Grisbrooke, W. Jardine. "The Formative Period—Cathedral and Monastic Offices." In *The Study of Liturgy*, 403–420. New York: Oxford University Press, 1992.

Heiler, Friedrich. "Contemplation in Christian Mysticism." In *Spiritual Disciplines: Papers from the Eranos Yearbooks*, 186–238. Princeton: Princeton University Press, 1985.

Hope, D[avid] M. "Medieval Western Rites" in *The Study of Liturgy*, 264–285. New York: Oxford University Press, 1992.

Jaffé, Aniela. "Symbolism in the Visual Arts." In *Man and His Symbols.* Edited by Carl Jung, 255–322. New York: Dell Publishing, 1968.

Klauser, Theodor. *A Short History of the Western Liturgy.* 1965. Eng. trans. Oxford: Oxford University Press, 1979.

Knowles, David, OSB. *Christian Monasticism*. New York: World University Library, 1969.

Leeuw, Gerardus van der. *Sacred and Profane Beauty: The Holy in Art*. New York: Holt, Rinehart and Winston, 1963.

Morris, Colin. "Christian Civilization 1050-1400." In *Oxford Illustrated History of Christianity*, 196–232. Oxford: Oxford University Press, 1990.

Radding, Charles. *A World Made by Men: Cognition and Society, 400-1200*. Chapel Hill: University of North Carolina Press, 1985.

Ratcliff, E. C. "The Choir Offices." In *Liturgy and Worship*, 257–295. London: SPCK, 1954.

Steiner, Ruth. "The Music for a Cluny Office of St. Benedict. In *Monasticism and the Arts*, 81–113. Syracuse: Syracuse University Press, 1984.

Taft, Robert, SJ. *The Liturgy of the Hours*. Collegeville, Minn.: The Liturgical Press, 1986.

Wright, Craig. *Music and Ceremony at Notre Dame, 500-1500*. Cambridge: Cambridge University Press, 1989.

Chapter 3

"Anglican Chant." In *The Oxford Companion to Music*, 32–35. London: Oxford University Press, 1972.

Batiffol, Pierre. *History of the Roman Breviary*. London: Longmans, Green, 1912.

Bonta, Stephen. "Liturgical Problems in Monteverdi's Marian Vespers." *Journal of the American Musicological Society* 20 (1967): 87-106.

Chadwick, Owen, ed. *Western Asceticism.* Philadelphia: The Westminster Press, 1958.

Dixon, Graham. "Handel's Music for the Carmelites." *Early Music* 15 (1987): 16- 29.

——————. "Monteverdi's Vespers of 1610: della Beata Virgine?" *Early Music* 15 (1987): 386-389.

Egeria: Diary of a Pilgrimage, trans. George E. Gingras. New York: Newman Press, 1970.

Ellinwood, Leonard. "From Plainsong to Anglican Chant." In *Cantors at the Crossroads,* 21–24. St. Louis: Concordia, 1967.

Evans, Joan. *Monastic Life at Cluny 910-1157.* London: Oxford University Press, 1931.

Fenlon, Iain. "The Monteverdi Vespers: Suggested Answers to Some Fundamental Questions." *Early Music* 5 (1977): 380-387.

Gelineau, Joseph, SJ. "Music and Singing in the Liturgy." In *The Study of Liturgy,* 493–507. New York: Oxford University Press, 1992.

Grisbrooke, W. Jardine. "The Formative Period—Cathedral and Monastic Offices." In *The Study of Liturgy,* 403–420. New York: Oxford University Press, 1992.

Hiley, David. *Western Plainchant:* Oxford: Oxford University Press, 1993.

Hunt, Noreen. *Cluny Under Saint Hugh 1049-1109.* London: Edward Arnold, 1967.

Jungmann, Joseph A., SJ. *Christian Prayer Through the Centuries.* 1969. Eng. trans. New York: Paulist Press, 1978.

Knowles, David, OSB. *Christian Monasticism.* New York: World University Library, 1969.

le Huray, Peter. "Anglican Chant." *The New Grove Dictionary of Music and Musicians.* London: Macmillan, 1980.

McKinnon, James, ed. *Music and Society: Antiquity and the Middle Ages.* Englewood Cliffs, N.J.: Prentice Hall, 1990.

Mayr-Harting, Henry. "The West: the Age of Conversion." In *Oxford Illustrated History of Christianity.* Oxford: Oxford University Press, 1990.

—————. *Music in Early Christian Literature.* Cambridge: Cambridge University Press, 1987.

Ratcliff, E. C. "The Choir Offices." In *Liturgy and Worship,* 257–295. London: SPCK, 1954.

Saenger, Paul. "Silent Reading: Its Impact on Late Medieval Script and Society." *Viator: Medieval and Renaissance Studies* 13 (1982): 367-414.

Shepherd, John. "Music, Text and Subjectivity." In *Music as a Social Text,* 174–185. Cambridge: Polity Press, 1991.

Steiner, Ruth. "The Music for a Cluny Office of St. Benedict. In *Monasticism and the Arts,* 81–113. Syracuse: Syracuse University Press, 1984.

Taft, Robert, SJ. *The Liturgy of the Hours.* Collegeville, Minn.: The Liturgical Press, 1986.

Wilson, Ruth Mack. "Anglican Chant and Chanting in England and America, 1660-1811." Ph.D. diss., University of Illinois, 1988.

Wilson, Tim. [audiotape] *Chant: the Healing Power of Voice and Ear.* Collegeville, Minn.: The Liturgical Press, [n.d.].

Chapter 4

Apel, Willi. *The History of Keyboard Music to 1700.* Bloomington: Indiana University Press, 1972.

Bonta, Stephen. "The Uses of the Sonata da Chiesa." *Journal of the American Musicological Society* 22 (1969): 54-84.

Bradshaw, Paul. *The Search for the Origins of Christian Worship.* New York: Oxford University Press, 1992.

Bynum, Caroline Walker. *Holy Feast and Holy Fast: the Religious Significance of Food to Medieval Women.* Berkeley: University of California Press, 1987.

Crocker, Richard. *The Early Medieval Sequence.* Berkeley: University of California Press, 1977.

Croegaert, A. *The Mass: A Liturgical Commentary.* Westminster, Md.: The Newman Press, 1958.

Dahl, Nils A. "Anamnesis: Memory and Commemoration in Early Christianity." In *Jesus in the Memory of the Early Church*, 11–29. Minneapolis: Augsburg, 1976.

Fassler, Margot Elsbeth. *Gothic Song: Victorine sequences and Augustinian reform in twelfth-century Paris.* Cambridge: Cambridge University Press, 1993.

Gingras, George E. trans., *Egeria: Diary of a Pilgrimage.* New York: Newman Press, 1970.

"The Golden Proportion: A Conversation between Richard Temple and Keith Critchlow." *Parabola* 16, no. 4 (1991): 28-36.

Harper, John. *The Forms and Orders of Western Liturgy from the Tenth to the Eighteenth Century.* Oxford: Oxford University Press, 1991.

Hammond, Frederick. *Girolamo Frescobaldi.* Cambridge: Harvard University Press, 1983.

Heiler, Friedrich. "Contemplation in Christian Mysticism." In *Spiritual Disciplines: Papers from the Eranos Yearbooks,* 186–238. Princeton: Princeton University Press, 1985.

Hiley, David. *Western Plainchant.* Oxford: Oxford University Press, 1993.

Hope, D[avid] M. "Medieval Western Rites" in *The Study of Liturgy,* 264–285. New York: Oxford University Press, 1992.

Jeremias, Joachim. *The Eucharistic Words of Jesus,* trans. Norman Perrin. London: SCM, 1966.

Jung, Carl. "Transformation Symbols in the Mass." In *Psychology and Western Religion,* 97–192. Princeton: Princeton University Press, 1984.

Jungmann, SJ, Joseph A. *The Mass of the Roman Rite: Its Origins and Development.* 2 vols. 1949. Eng. trans. New York: Benziger Bros., 1951.

Klauser, Theodor. *A Short History of the Western Liturgy.* 1965. Eng. trans. Oxford: Oxford University Press, 1979.

Markus, Robert. "From Rome to the Barbarian Kingdoms (330-700)." In *Oxford Illustrated History of Christianity,* 62–91. Oxford: Oxford University Press, 1990.

McKinnon, James. *Music and Society: Antiquity and the Middle Ages.* Englewood Cliffs, N.J.: Prentice Hall, 1990.

_____. *Music in Early Christian Literature.* Cambridge: Cambridge University Press, 1987.

_____. "On the Question of Psalmody in the Ancient Synagogue." *Early Music History* 6 (1986): 159-191.

Moore, James H. "The Liturgical Use of the Organ in Seventeenth-Century Italy: New Documents, New Hypotheses." In *Frescobaldi Studies,* 351–383. Durham: Duke University Press, 1987.

Ordo Romanus Primus. Edited by E. G. Cuthbert F. Atchley. In *The Library of Liturgiology & Ecclesiology for English Readers.* London: The De la More Press, 1905.

Roesner, Edward. "The Performance of Parisian Organum." *Early Music* 7 (1979): 174-189.

Schnoebelen, Anne. "The Role of the Violin in the Resurgence of the Mass in the 17th Century." *Early Music* 18 (1990): 537-542.

Smith, John A. "The Ancient Synagogue, the Early Church and Singing." *Music and Letters* 65 (1984): 1-16.

van Deusen, Nancy. *The Harp and the Soul.* Lewiston, N.Y.: Edwin Mellen Press, 1989.

Wright, Craig. *Music and Ceremony at Notre Dame, 500-1500.* Cambridge: Cambridge University Press, 1989.

Wybrew, Hugh. "The Setting of the Liturgy: 'Ceremonial'." In *The Study of Liturgy,* 485–93. New York: Oxford University Press, 1992.

Chapter 5

[Andrewes, Lancelot]. *Ninety-six Sermons by the Right Honourable and Reverend Father in God, Lancelot Andrewes.* Oxford: John Henry Parker, 1841.

Bikle, Charles A. "A Brief Analysis of Three Sermons Preached on St. Cecilia's Day in London During the 1690's." In *Music from the Middle Ages through the Twentieth Century: Essays in Honor of Gwynn S. McPeek*, 175–189. New York: Gordon and Breach, 1988.

Blume, Friedrich. *Protestant Church Music: A History.* New York: W. W. Norton, 1974.

Boyd, Malcolm. *Bach.* London: Dent, 1983.

Bumpus, John. *A History of English Cathedral Music.* London: T. Werner Laurie, [n.d.].

Butler, Gregory. "Music and Rhetoric in Early Seventeenth-Century English Sources." *Musical Quarterly* 66 (1980): 53-64.

Chandos, John. *In God's Name.* Indianapolis: Bobbs-Merrill, 1971.

David, Hans, and Arthur Mendel, eds. *The Bach Reader.* New York: W. W. Norton, 1966.

[Donne, John]. *Donne's Sermons: Selected Passages with an Essay by Logan Pearsall Smith.* Oxford: Clarendon, 1919.

Leaver, Robin A. "Bach and Pietism." *Concordia Theological Quarterly* 55(1991): 5- 22.

_____, ed. *J. S. Bach and Scripture: Glosses from the Calov Bible Commentary.* St. Louis: Concordia, 1985.

_____. *J. S. Bach as Preacher: His Passions and Music in Worship*. St. Louis: Concordia, 1982.

_____. "The Liturgical Place and Homiletic Purpose of Bach's Cantatas." *Worship* 59 (1985): 194-202.

Mitchell, W. Fraser. *English Pulpit Oratory from Andrewes to Tillotson: A Study of its Literary Aspects*. London: SPCK, 1932.

Pelikan, Jaroslav. *Bach Among the Theologians*. Philadelphia: Fortress Press, 1986.

Richardson, Caroline Francis. *English Preachers and Preaching*. New York: Macmillan, 1928.

Spitta, Philip. *Johann Sebastian Bach. 1889*. Eng. trans. New York: Dover, 1951.

Stiller, Günther. *Johann Sebastian Bach and Liturgical Life in Leipzig*. Trans. Herbert J. A. Bouman, Daniel F. Poclott, Hilton C. Oswald, ed. Robin A. Leaver. St. Louis: Concordia, 1984.

Watson, Foster. *The English Grammar Schools to 1660: their Curriculum and Practice*. Cambridge: Cambridge University Press, 1908.

Westrup, J. A. *Purcell*. New York: Collier, 1962.

Winn, James. *John Dryden and His World*. New Haven: Yale University Press, 1987.

Zimmerman, Franklin. *The Anthems of Henry Purcell*. New York: American Choral Foundation, 1971.

_____. *Henry Purcell 1659-1695: His Life and Times*. Philadelphia: University of Pennsylvania Press, 1983.

Chapter 6

Burrows, David. *Sound, Speech, and Music.* Amherst: University of Massachusetts Press, 1990.

Lovejoy, Arthur. *The Great Chain of Being.* Cambridge, Mass.: 1936.

Shepherd, John. "Music, Text and Subjectivity." In *Music as a Social Text,* 174–85. Cambridge: Polity Press, 1991.

Tillyard, E[ustace] M[andeville] W[etenhall]. *The Elizabethan World Picture.* New York: Vintage Books, [n.d.].

INDEX